THE ANCIENT AMERICAN WORLD

RONALD MELLOR &
AMANDA H. PODANY
GENERAL EDITORS

THE ANCIENT AMERICAN WORLD

William Fash & Mary E. Lyons

OXFORD
UNIVERSITY PRESS

For my sons, Bill, Nate, and Ben, who as children longed for a book on the ancient Americas —WF

For Eileen, Gene, and Patrick, who took care of business so that I could write —ML

OXFORD
UNIVERSITY PRESS

Oxford University Press, Inc., publishes works that further Oxford University's objective of excellence in research, scholarship, and education.

Oxford   New York
Auckland   Cape Town   Dar es Salaam   Hong Kong   Karachi   Kuala Lumpur   Madrid   Melbourne
Mexico City   Nairobi   New Delhi   Shanghai   Taipei   Toronto

With offices in
Argentina   Austria   Brazil   Chile   Czech Republic   France   Greece   Guatemala   Hungary   Italy
Japan   Poland   Portugal   Singapore   South Korea   Switzerland   Thailand   Turkey   Ukraine   Vietnam

Copyright © 2005 by Oxford University Press, Inc.

Published by Oxford University Press, Inc.
198 Madison Avenue, New York, New York 10016
www.oup.com

Oxford is a registered trademark of Oxford University Press

Library of Congress Cataloging-in-Publication Data

Fash, William Leonard.
  The ancient American world / William Fash & Mary E. Lyons.
    p. cm.—(The world in ancient times)
  Includes bibliographical references and index.
  ISBN-13: 978-0-19-517465-6 — ISBN 978-0-19-522247-0 (Calif. ed.) — ISBN 978-019-522242-5 (set)
  ISBN-10: 0-19-517465-8 — 0-19-522247-4 (Calif. ed.) — ISBN 0-19-522242-3 (set)
   1. Indians of Mexico—History—Sources.   2. Indians of Mexico—Social life and customs.   3. Indians of Mexico—Antiquities.   4. Indians of South America—History—Sources.   5. Indians of South America—Social life and customs.   6. Indians of South America—Antiquities.   7. Mexico—Antiquities.   8. South America—Antiquities.   I. Lyons, Mary E.   II. Title.   III. Series.
  F1219.F27 2005
  972'.01—dc22

                              2004020711

9 8 7 6 5 4 3 2 1

Printed in the United States of America
on acid-free paper

Design: Stephanie Blumenthal
Layout: Mary Neal Meador
Cover design and logo: Nora Wertz

On the cover: The statue (center) is a portrait of a dignitary from the South American kingdom of Wari from around 750 CE. The glyphs (left) are from the Dresden Codex, a Maya bark-paper book containing farmers' almanacs and astronomical tables.
Frontispiece: The back side of the 15th century highland Mexican Codex Cospi describes rituals that people carried out to obtain good luck and protection.

**RONALD MELLOR &
AMANDA H. PODANY**

GENERAL EDITORS

DIANE L. BROOKS, Ed.D.

EDUCATION CONSULTANT

The Early Human World
Peter Robertshaw & Jill Rubalcaba

The Ancient Near Eastern World
Amanda H. Podany & Marni McGee

The Ancient Egyptian World
Eric H. Cline & Jill Rubalcaba

The Ancient South Asian World
Jonathan Mark Kenoyer & Kimberley Heuston

The Ancient Chinese World
Terry Kleeman & Tracy Barrett

The Ancient Greek World
Jennifer T. Roberts & Tracy Barrett

The Ancient Roman World
Ronald Mellor & Marni McGee

The Ancient American World
William Fash & Mary E. Lyons

**The World in Ancient Times:
Primary Sources and Reference Volume**
Ronald Mellor & Amanda H. Podany

CONTENTS

A 〔❝〕 marks each chapter's primary sources—ancient writings and artifacts that "speak" to us from the past.

CAST OF CHARACTERS

Because The World in Ancient Times *covers many cultures, we use the abbreviations* CE *for "Common Era" and* BCE *for "Before the Common Era." The traditional equivalents are* BC *for "Before Christ" and* AD *for "Anno Domini," Latin for "In the Year of Our Lord," referring to the birth of Jesus Christ.*

Atahualpa (ah-tah-WHAL-pa), about 1500–1534 CE • last Inca emperor

Bol (BOWL), about 775–825 CE • Maya scribe of Aguateca

Cieza de León, Pedro de (PEH-dro deh see-EH-sah deh leh-OWN), 1522–1554 CE • Spanish chronicler of the Inca world

Cortés, Hernán (err-NAHN cor-TESS), 1485–1547 CE • explorer who conquered Aztec empire for Spain

Díaz, Bernal (bear-NAHL DEE-ahz), 1495–1584 CE • Spanish foot soldier who described conquest of Mexico

Guamán Poma (gwa-MAHN PO-mah), about 1580–1620 CE • native South American who wrote about and drew pictures of Inca world

Huayna Capac (WHY-nah KAH-pahk), about 1460–1527 CE • powerful late Inca emperor

Itzcoatl (EETZ-ko-aht), about 1380–1440 CE • Aztec emperor who forged the Triple Alliance empire

K'inich Yax K'uk' Mo' (KUH-een-eech yahsh KUH-oo-kuh MO-uh), about 370–435 CE • first king of Copán, originally named K'uk Mo' Ajaw (KUH-oo-kuh MO-uh, ah-HOW)

Janaab' Pakal I (OO-nahb PAH-kahl) the first, 603–683 CE • Maya ruler of Palenque

Lady Sak K'uk' (SAHK kuh-OOK), about 580–640 CE • queen of Palenque; mother of Pakal I

Malintzin (mahl-EEN-tzeen), about 1500–1551 CE • Nahua native interpreter for Cortés during conquest of Mexico

Mitmaq (MEET-mahk), about 1450–1534 CE • Inca colonizers and displaced peoples

Moctezuma II (MOCK-teh-ZOO-mah) the second, about 1467–1520 CE • Aztec emperor captured by Spaniards

One Earthquake, about 530–500 BCE • war captive and sacrificial victim of Zapotec rulers of San José Mogote, Mexico

Pachacuti (pah-chah-KOO-tee), about 1420–1471 CE • first Inca emperor

Pizarro, Francisco (fran-CEASE-co pee-SAHR-ro), about 1500–1560 CE • conquistador who took over Inca Empire for Spain

Quetzalcoatl (ket-zahl-CO-aht) • an important Mesoamerican god; also name of great Toltec ruler about 750–800 CE

Sahagún, Bernardino de (ber-nar-DEE-no deh sa-ah-GOON), 1499–1590 • Spanish missionary whose mastery of the Aztec language (Nahuatl) enabled him to write the greatest chronicle, earning him the title of "the first Anthropologist"

Smoking Mirror • "first among all the gods" in Mesoamerica; followers defeated Quetzalcoatl in Tula about 850 CE

Taycanamu (tay-cah-NAH-mu), about 1300–1350 CE • founder of the Andean Kingdom of Chimor

Gulf of Mexico

Isla Cerritos — Cozumel

Caribbean Sea

CENTRAL AMERICA

•Chichén Itzá

Yucatán
Peninsula

Calakmul
El Mirador•
Tikal
Tabasco •
Bone (Palenque)

La Venta
Aguateca

Teotihuacan•
Tenochtitlan•
San Lorenzo
San José Mogote• •Monte Albán
•Copán

Quito•

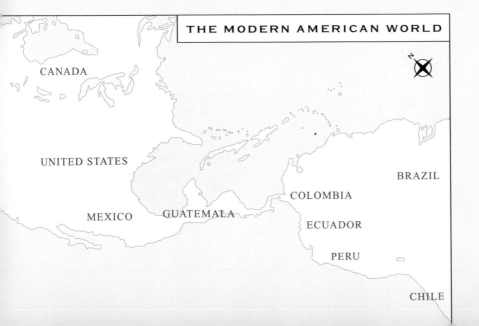

THE MODERN AMERICAN WORLD

Pacific Ocean

CANADA

UNITED STATES

BRAZIL

COLOMBIA

MEXICO   GUATEMALA

ECUADOR

PERU

CHILE

THE ANCIENT AMERICAN WORLD

0 _____ 400 mi
0 _____ 600 km

SOUTH AMERICA

rca
pán   •Chavín
an •Cerro
an Blanco   •Wari   •Cuzco   •Tiwanaku
                        Lake Titicaca

Moche River

Andes Mountains

SOME PRONUNCIATIONS

Aguateca (ah-gwah-TEH-kah)

Calakmul (kah-lahk-MUHL)

Caxamarca (kah-ha-MAHR-kah)

Cerro Blanco (SER-ro BLAHN-ko)

Chan Chan (chahn chahn)

Chavín (chah-VEEN)

Chichén Itzá (chih-CHEHN eet-ZAH)

Copán (koh-PAHN)

Cozumel (koh-zoo-MEHL)

Cuzco (KOOZ-ko)

El Mirador (ehl meer-ah-DOR)

Isla Cerritos (EES-lah seh-REE-tos)

Moche (MOH-chay)

Monte Albán (MOHN-te ahl-BAHN)

Oaxaca (wah-HAH-kuh)

Palenque (pah-LEHN-kay)

Quito (KEE-to)

San José Mogote (san ho-ZAY moh-GOH-tay)

San Lorenzo (san loh-REHN-zoh)

Sipán (see-PAHN)

Tabasco (toh-BA-sko)

Tenochtitlan (teh-noch-TEET-lahn)

Teotihuacan (tay-oh-tee-HWAH-kahn)

Tikal (tee-KAHL)

Titicaca (TIH-tih-KAH-kah)

Tiwanaku (TEE-wan-AH-koo)

Tula (TOO-luh)

Wari (WAH-ree)

Yucatán (yoo-ka-TAHN)

INTRODUCTION
WHAT'S UNDER YOUR BEDROOM?

archaeo + *logy* = "ancient" + "speech" in Greek—that is, discussion of ancient things. Archaeologists are people who study ancient history by looking at evidence such as graves, buildings, tools, and pottery.

Think about your bedroom. What if a future **archaeologist** investigated it in 5000 CE? Would she find the remains of a compact disc or a crumpled soda can? An unmade bed or dirty sock?

Maybe under your house or apartment building she'd uncover a hoe, left by a long-ago farmer. After digging deeper, she might discover a stone tool made by an ancient artist. Even deeper, and her trowel could hit the skull of a prehistoric animal that ambled through what was once your neighborhood. It kind of makes you wonder: what *is* under your bedroom, anyway?

That same curiosity drives archaeologists. They look for ruins of great temples, palaces, and roads. They keep an eye out for trash and treasure: leftovers from a cooked meal, perhaps, or broken pots buried with a skeleton.

Whatever is deep under your bedroom has probably been there for a long time. And if you live anywhere in the Americas—North, Central, or South—"how long" is a question that people have debated for years. Scholars think that native people came from Asia 13,000 years ago. Some arrived by sea. Others walked overland across a land bridge that once connected Asia with Alaska but is now covered with water. In less than 1,000 years, various groups wandered into Alaska and spread across northern Canada. Some were restless and kept going all the way down to the southern tip of South America.

Eventually, the nomads settled down and built cities with leaders, governments, and shared religions: the ingredients of civilization.

The civilizations you'll read about first in this book developed in Mexico and parts of Central America—the area that archaeologists call Mesoamerica.

MIDDLE NAME

In 1941, a scholar was studying the land between North and South America. He realized that people in much of the region shared the same ancient culture: pyramids, a rubber ball game, complicated calendars, and bark-paper books. They also worshipped similar gods and ate the same kinds of food. The scholar named the area Mesoamerica, which comes from *mesos*, a Greek word meaning middle.

Archaeologists name a civilization after the people who built it or for the name of its main city. Mesoamerican civilizations include the Olmec people, the city of Teotihuacan, the Toltec people, various **Maya** tribes, and a collection of different tribes under the one name of Aztec.

In South America, the oldest civilizations developed in present-day Peru, Bolivia, Chile, Argentina, and Ecuador. Archaeologists call them Andean civilizations, because the Andes Mountains run north and south through this part of the world. The earliest Andean civilizations include the cities of Chavín, Tiwanaku, and Wari. Later ones are named for the Moche, Chimú, and Inca peoples.

When Spaniards first encountered the Aztec and Maya civilizations in the 16th century, they were astonished to see thousands of books written in **hieroglyphs**. In the Andean world, Spanish explorer Francisco Pizarro was amazed by incredible feats of engineering, such as woven reed bridges that spanned deep mountain chasms. He didn't find books, because Andean people never developed a writing system. But they had little use for writing, anyway. Each generation carefully memorized Andean myths, legends, and history, word for word.

The Spaniards brought a few great ideas of their own to the Americas. For some reason, Mesoamericans had never come up with the idea of using wheels for transportation. And they had no beasts of burden such as horses, mules, and donkeys. Wheeled wagons and pack animals were a boon to Mesoamericans, who had always hauled loads by hand.

Unfortunately, the Spaniards also brought intolerance. During what we call the Spanish conquest, Spaniards forced native people to serve the Spanish king. Spaniards worshipped the Christian god, so native people had to erase all traces of earlier religions and become Christians. Anyone who refused was enslaved or killed. To make certain that native people forgot their religion, one Spanish priest burned almost all the Maya books in blazing bonfires.

The book burning was a tragedy, but not everything was lost. The Maya managed to hide a few volumes, and some priests took others, which ended up in Europe. Archaeol-

People often confuse *Maya* with Mayan. Maya refers to a group of people. *Mayan* is the language that Maya people speak. Say it three times, and you'll never forget it: The *Maya* speak, read, and write *Mayan*.

hiero + *glyph* = "sacred" + "carving" in ancient Greek. Hieroglyphs are signs that stand for an idea, a word, or a syllable. A single sign is a glyph.

GLYPH GLOSSARY?

Glyphs are complicated. Not only do today's experts argue heatedly about how to interpret them, but even the early native historians disagreed about them. Ancient American scribes who wrote glyphs for the Codex Mendoza argued for days about the meaning of their own writing!

MANY TONGUES

After the Spanish conquest of the Americas, some native people refused to forget their languages. In central Mexico, most people speak Spanish, but others know only Nahuatl, the language of their ancestors. In Guatemala, many Maya tribes still speak one of 39 ancient Mayan tongues. And the ancient Quechua language is still alive and well in Peru.

ogists call these the native chronicles, or histories, because native people wrote them before the conquest. Every day, modern scholars use them to figure out the meaning of another Mayan glyph.

During the conquest, many people held tightly to their customs and history. For decades afterward, Spanish priests watched and listened to native people and recorded their history. Some native people learned to read and write their own language using our alphabet. They recorded their history, too. Scholars call all these books the colonial chronicles, because they were written after Spain turned parts of the Americas into colonies.

The colonial chronicles are not always accurate. The Spaniards usually put themselves in the best light when writing about the conquest. Native historians also fudged on the truth. Like the Spaniards, they wanted their history to sound glorious, even when it wasn't. Truthful or not, the colonial chronicles are the only written records we have from the time of the conquest.

As you read these words, some historian is reading the chronicles, trying to separate falsehood from fact. Somewhere a team of archaeologists is digging up bones or pieces of pottery. And an epigrapher—a person who studies ancient writing—is staring at a glyph, trying to figure out what it means. All three kinds of information help scholars uncover the hidden story of the ancient Americas.

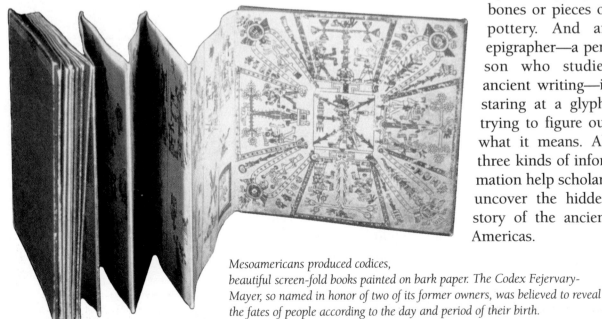

Mesoamericans produced codices, beautiful screen-fold books painted on bark paper. The Codex Fejervary-Mayer, so named in honor of two of its former owners, was believed to reveal the fates of people according to the day and period of their birth.

CHAPTER 1

PEOPLE OF MAIZE
EARLY FARMERS IN THE VALLEY OF OAXACA

⌜❝⌝ A JAR FROM MEXICO,
POPOL VUH,
FRAY BERNARDINO
DE SAHAGÚN, AND
THE FLORENTINE
CODEX

The ancient Mesoamerican rain god was a very moody fellow—or so people thought. Sometimes he was too quiet. This was a worrisome sign. It meant that drought would shrivel the crops and dry up the fields. Other times, he roared like a dragon and threw fire that snaked across the sky. The people put up with the god's foul temper, because thunder and lightning were signs that life-giving rain was on the way. As long as the rain god didn't send killing floods, crops would grow, and they would survive.

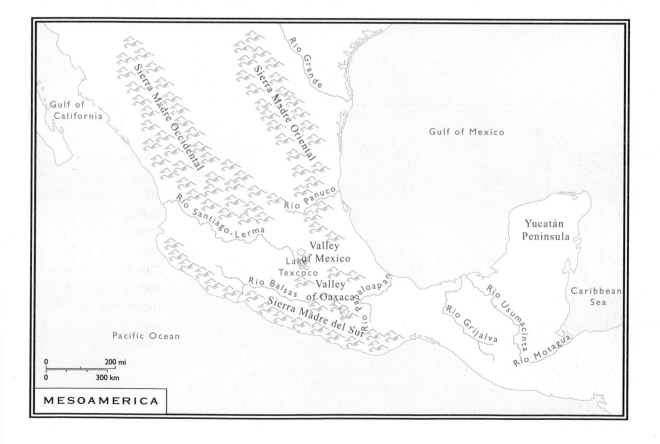

MESOAMERICA

Local workers examine a dark patch of soil in the remains of an ancient Zapotec house in Oaxaca, Mexico. Though the walls and roof disintegrated long ago, archaeologists found ancient tools below the surface of the soil.

`[66]` Pottery jar with Sky Dragon image, Mexico, 1000 BCE

Floods and drought were common when ancient Mesoamericans first began growing maize, or wild corn, around 5000 BCE. And archaeological digs prove that by 900 BCE fickle weather still controlled their fate.

Since the 1970s, archaeologists have been digging in an area of Mesoamerica called the Valley of Oaxaca. They've located the remains of 22 houses in 5 ancient villages. In every single house, they've found pieces of large pottery jars. One archaeologist discovered a pottery bowl with a simple carving on the outside. After an artist drew the carved design on paper, the archaeologist saw the face of an angry Sky Dragon glaring back at him. The god's flaming eyebrows and sharp teeth tell a story: ancient Mesoamericans tried to please the rain god by carving his face on pottery.

Designs on pottery tell only part of the story of ancient Mesoamerica. While digging in Oaxaca, archaeologists unearthed what was left of a thatched-roof hut. The house was about 16 feet wide and 10 feet deep. Buried in the rubble were hunting, cooking, and sewing tools. Finding the tools was one thing. Figuring out who used them was another. For that, the archaeologists turned to old books.

In the 16th century CE, Mesoamericans wrote codices, or handwritten books, that described tasks performed by

men and women. Mesoamerican women had always prepared and cooked the food, spun and woven cloth, and
made storage jars. "The good weaver of designs is skilled—
a maker of vari-colored capes, an outliner of designs, a
blender of colors, a joiner of pieces, a matcher of pieces, a
person of good memory." Men had always built the houses, planted and harvested maize, shucked kernels from
cobs, made tools, and hunted deer. "The farmer prepares
the soil . . . harvests the maize stalks, gathers the stubble;
he removes the tassels, gathers the green maize ears, breaks
off the ripened ears."

This written record helped the archaeologists make
sense of where they found the tools. To the right of the
doorway, they uncovered tools for a woman's tasks: pots,
spindles, and sewing needles. On the left side, they excavated tools for a man's tasks: deer-bone scrapers, stones,
and obsidian blades. In the middle of the house, they found
both kinds of tools.

The archaeologists also knew that modern people in the
Valley of Oaxaca still divide their work areas in the same
fashion. By combining this knowledge with written clues
and evidence from the ground, they could make an educated guess about early Mesoamerican activities: men worked
to the left of the door, and women to the right. And sometimes they shared tasks in the middle of the hut.

Both the Sky Dragon jar and the tools will help you picture life in ancient Mesoamerica. Think of a **hypothetical** village in 900 BCE. Six families have built a cluster of huts on the
flat valley floor. Each family would be raising chili peppers,
tomatoes, and avocados in a garden plot next to their house.
In nearby fields, bean and squash vines might sprawl lazily
beneath six-foot-tall maize plants. Elsewhere, mesquite bushes and prickly pear cactus would be growing willy-nilly.

From their digging, archaeologists know that early Mesoamerican houses faced one another in a rough circle.
That would make it easy to walk outside, scan the sky, and
chat with a neighbor about the weather. On a sunny day,
families in this village could have seen mountains soaring
8,000 feet high in the blue distance.

Fray Bernardino de Sahagún,
Florentine Codex, 16th
century CE

Fray Bernardino de Sahagún,
Florentine Codex, 16th
century CE

hypo + *thesis* = "under" +
"placing," or "basis" or "foundation" in ancient Greek.
Hypothetical means "sup-
posed or imagined as the
basis of an argument."
Archaeologists and historians
use evidence they have found
to create a hypothetical, or
supposed, picture of the past.

THE THREE SISTERS

Mesoamericans raised maize, squash, and beans in ancient times, and they still eat these staple foods today. They call them the Three Sisters, because the plants grow so well together. Beans planted underneath maize plants climb up the tall stalks. Squash planted in the same mound spreads leaves that hold moisture in the soil. The Three Sisters fill many nutritional needs. Maize contains carbohydrates, beans are full of protein, and squash is rich in vitamin A.

Native people also still raise tomatoes, avocadoes, and chili peppers. Avocado is the main ingredient in guacamole, and salsa is made with tomatoes and chilies. If you've ever eaten a taco—a folded tortilla shell stuffed with tomatoes, guacamole, and salsa—you know these foods pack a lot of flavor. As an extra bonus, they also contain a generous amount of vitamin C.

Suppose that the house the archaeologists excavated was still standing. And let's say you could step through the doorway. Today a curtain of rain would be falling, so everyone is indoors. The windowless room is dark, but you can hear sounds of work and conversation.

When your eyes adjust, you might see a boy to the left of the doorway. He's holding a corn-shucker that his father cut from the foot bone of a deer. The child deftly removes two husks from a cob the size of a pen cap. Using the same tool, he scrapes off black, red, yellow, and white kernels.

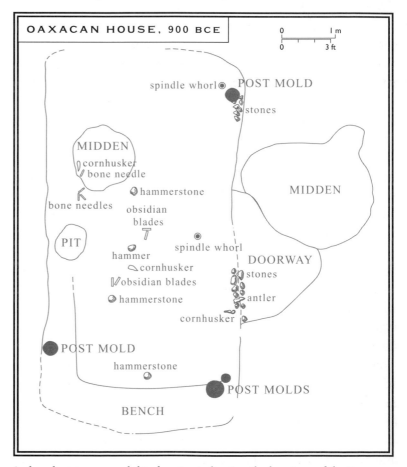

Archaeologists prepared this drawing indicating the locations of the items they found at a hut in Oaxaca. These include tools, post molds (the soil stains from the decomposed wood where supporting wooden posts stood), and middens, or garbage dumps. People threw leftover bones and ashes from cooking fires into their middens.

These tooth-breaking seeds are smaller versions of ones you see on corn on the cob.

To the right of the door, a mother is grinding kernels on a flat hammer stone. She scoops the crushed cornmeal into a five-gallon storage jar that she's hand-molded from clay. She has decorated the jar with a carving of a Sky Dragon—the grumpy rain god who can send too much rain or not enough.

The mother probably grinds maize from three to eight hours every day—that job is never done. With a handful of meal and water, she mixes tortilla dough. Then she cooks the thin, round cakes on a grill that sits in the corner.

A daughter may be working near the mother. This morning she could have started weaving a basket with a needle made of deer bone. Now she's wrapping softened plant fibers around a spindle and twirling it with both hands. The motion twists the fibers into thread she can later weave into cloth.

If you could walk across the room, you might see the father place a piece of black volcanic glass called obsidian on a hammer stone. He strikes the glass with a rock, and a sharp obsidian flake falls off. Settling on a nearby bench, he drapes a scrap of leather over one thigh and shapes the flake with a piece of deer antler.

As the rain falls harder, this father might stop his work and mutter something about the maize crop. Maize was so essential to early Mesoamericans' existence that they made up a myth about it. In the 17th century CE, an unnamed group of Mesoamericans wrote down this ancient myth in a book called the *Popol Vuh*. "Of yellow corn and of white corn they [the gods] made . . . flesh," the myth says. "Of cornmeal dough they made the arms and the legs of man." This family not only ate maize—they thought they *were* maize.

If only the Sky Dragon would cooperate! Last year, there may have been heavy rain in our hypothetical village. The downpours would have turned the maize fields to slimy mud. Most of the seedlings rotted in the ground, and bugs and birds greedily devoured the rest. Perhaps cloudbursts destroyed the vegetable garden, too, and the people of maize almost starved. This year, swollen black clouds have

LATER, IN NEW MEXICO

From 850 to 1250 CE, six to ten thousand Native Americans lived in Chaco Canyon, New Mexico. Scientists have found ancient corncobs on the site and compared them with ones from distant fields. The cobs suggest that these people grew their maize 50 miles away, perhaps because the canyon climate was too dry and cold for raising crops. They harvested the maize, then hand-carried it over steep bluffs back to the canyon.

❝ *Popol Vuh*, 17th century CE

dropped rain every afternoon. Today's storm is even more violent than usual.

When archaeologists excavated this hut, they discovered that it sat on a clay platform only two inches above the ground. Let's suppose that floodwater spilled over the doorway. The parents would have exchanged worried glances, dropped their tools, and urged the children to head for the nearest hillside.

The archaeologists also found a pit where the family kept jars of cornmeal. Just before fleeing, the mother and father would have grabbed these containers of precious food. As the family raced up the slope, they might have turned and looked back. They would have seen raging floodwaters snatch all five houses. Perhaps other villages in the Valley of Oaxaca survived such a flood, but the walls and roofs of these five huts would have been swept away. Only the abandoned tools remained, buried in mud and waiting for archaeologists to uncover them almost 3,000 years later.

It's possible that the hypothetical family survived on cornmeal until the rainstorms finally ended. Shaken by the experience, they would have protected themselves from other flash floods the Sky Dragon might send. The son would have helped his father dig into the hill, level a small plot of land, and create a terrace. Then they would have built a house on the terrace, wedging a stone wall in front to keep it from sliding down the slope during heavy rain. When the ground was dry enough, they would have planted a garden on the valley floor.

The following year, the skies might have been stubbornly blue, and the garden soil would have cracked like dry skin. The family would have known what to do, because they had lived through drought before. Archaeologists know that ancient Mesoamericans

A Zapotec farmer irrigates his field with water drawn from a 10-foot-deep well. This method of pot irrigation has produced the healthy crop of maize in the background.

used pot irrigation: they dug wells, lowered pots, and hauled up water to irrigate their crops. Terraces and pot irrigation show that the people of maize were very resourceful. They had to be, or they would starve or drown.

Eventually, people in the Valley of Oaxaca became efficient-enough farmers that they often had extra maize left over at the end of a growing season. They developed other food sources by taming turkeys, ducks, and rabbits. They even captured young deer that grazed in nearby maize fields. As deer became accustomed to humans, it was easy to lure them toward the house with food, and then pen them in the yard. The deer probably snacked on tasty leaves from the garden, and occasionally humans made a meal from the deer. But in general, the arrangement worked well for all.

A dependable food supply gave the people of Oaxaca time for making luxury items. Someone invented a way to weave heavy cotton cloaks and decorate them with colorful embroidery. Then a clever family decided they could barter their surplus maize and gorgeous cloaks for other items they needed. Markets for extra goods sprang up in the Valley of Oaxaca and throughout Mesoamerica.

It was an ideal solution, because the geography of Mesoamerica is so varied that no one place could provide everything people needed. When traders on foot or in canoes arrived from the far corners of Mesoamerica, local markets turned into bigger ones.

Sometimes money really does grow on trees. Early Mesoamericans used seedpods from the cacao tree to make a scrumptious chocolate drink called **cacahuatl**. People had no money as we know it, but cacao pods were so desirable that merchants used them the way we use cash. Jade, gold, and cloaks were some other ancient forms of money.

Over time, village markets grew into towns with hundreds of people, and towns became cities of thousands. Cities led to shared stories and customs, leaders, a set of rules for behavior, and public gathering places. Thanks to a steady food supply, the people of maize were building their first civilization.

A DRINK FOR THE GODS

Our modern hot chocolate drink is made with cocoa, hot milk, and sugar. Ancient Mesoamericans mixed cocoa with cold water and chili powder. For extra spiciness, they stirred in powdered blossoms from the ear flower. They also used the root of the achiote bush, which deepened the flavor and added a reddish color. The result was so delicious that people thought the gods would enjoy it. Some Central Americans still make two chocolate drinks: one for themselves, and one they put in a "god pot," or a pottery vessel made especially for the gods.

cacahuatl (cah-CAH-what) = "cacao bean water" in Nahuatl, the language people spoke in ancient Mexico before the Spaniards arrived.

CHAPTER 2

LAND OF RUBBER
THE OLMEC CIVILIZATION

" AN OLMEC HEAD
AND AN OLMEC
THRONE

olmeca (oal-MEH-kah) =
"land of rubber" in Nahuatl.
The Olmec lived in a region
that produced rubber from
the sap of rubber trees.

PLAY BALL!

Mesoamericans played a rubber-ball game as early as 1300 BCE. Players wore protective gear, because the hard rubber balls weighed up to seven pounds and could cause severe injuries. Using their hips or knees, players bounced the ball off the sloping sides of a sunken court. Archaeologists don't know the rules of the game, only that it could last for days. Teams had good reason to play for a long time. They believed that the Lords of the Underworld—the gods of death—would get angry if the ball touched the ground. By keeping the ball in the air, players defeated the dark forces of famine, disease, and death.

Ann Cyphers was already feeling cheerful on that May morning in 1994. After four years of working in the Gulf Coast region of Mexico, this enthusiastic archaeologist had found a wealth of information. Her subject was the **Olmec**. These ancient Mesoamericans lived in the heart of rubber tree country. They are best known for colossal stone heads they chiseled from basalt, or volcanic rock, between 1200 and 600 BCE.

Researchers agree that the heads are images of Olmec leaders, but Cyphers wanted to learn about the lives of ordinary Olmecs. As she said in an interview, the heads are "huge and important, but you can't judge Olmec culture on . . . that one thing. It would be like judging America based on the White House."

So in 1990, Ann Cyphers traveled to San Lorenzo, a village in the heart of the Olmec civilization. San Lorenzo sits on a natural table of land called a plateau. For some unknown reason, the Olmec built the plateau even higher. Their man-made mountain rises 150 feet and stretches for three-quarters of a mile.

Archaeologists have long thought that Olmec leaders lived on the plateau, high above the forests and rivers. But what about ordinary Olmec? Where were their houses, and what did they do with themselves all day? Cyphers had a hunch that they lived on the terraced sides of the plateau.

Between 1990 and 1994, she tirelessly paced the slopes. It was a tough job. The Olmec lived so long ago that clues about their lives are hidden under centuries of debris. Cyphers could walk over an Olmec building and not even know it was buried deep under her feet. When she saw a stain in the soil or a pottery fragment lying on the ground, she suspected a building was under the surface. Slowly, despite mosquitoes, ticks, and six-foot-long poisonous snakes, she figured out where she should excavate.

The two years of planning paid off. On the terraced slopes, Cyphers uncovered mud-wall houses with outside hearths. Near each house, she found garbage pits filled with deer and dog bones—scraps from long-ago meals. And in every house, she saw fragments of stone sculptures or stone tools. This evidence of craft making proved that ordinary Olmec lived, cooked, and ate in the same place where they worked—in modern words, they had home offices.

Some craft activities took place right under the ruler's nose, where he could keep an eye on his workers. Near an Olmec ruler's palace on top of the plateau, Cyphers found more than two tons of stone beads: evidence of a bead workshop. In another area, she discovered numerous obsidian blades. These were proof that craftspeople produced the sharp tools in one place. In still another spot, she uncovered an assortment of basalt chips. She decided that this was where carvers made the giant heads.

Ancient builders at San Lorenzo stained the walls and sand floors of the Red Palace at San Lorenzo with red pigment, a color that was considered sacred. Stone columns and underground drains found in the palace are evidence that the Olmec were sophisticated architects and hydraulic engineers.

Cyphers remembers that when she started digging, the residents of San Lorenzo thought she was a "crazy foreign woman" searching for garbage. "The local people think that I'm a terrible archaeologist," she joked in a magazine interview, "because I haven't found a . . . colossal head." But her findings helped the residents of San Lorenzo see that everyday Olmec life was important, too.

Continued on page 26

ARCHAEOLOGIST AT WORK:
AN INTERVIEW WITH ANN CYPHERS

How did you become interested in archaeology?

I had the idea to study archaeology in high school. My hometown is located very close to Dixon Mound, in Ohio. The Dixon brothers had been building a barn, and they found burials. Instead of yanking things out, they decided to excavate the mound in their spare time. They left the burials in their actual positions, with the offerings, and even built sheds over the mound. My dad would go out there, and I'd tag along. I'd get to go into the building, because by this time it was a personal museum for the Dixons and open to the public. Mr. Dixon would take us down into the burial area. I'd spend hours down there.

What physical work do you do besides digging?

A lot of squatting, hauling, and toting. And we walk for surveying. You traverse the terrain looking for sites, mapping them, collecting the artifacts you find on the surface. This is very important, because from the pottery remains on the surface, you can date the site. Then you can say, "Oh, this site was occupied in 1800 BCE, then 1200 BCE, then 800 BCE."

What's the toughest thing about being an archaeologist?

Sometimes you don't get a hot shower. You have to take baths out of buckets.

How do you feel about the looting and illegal sale of Mesoamerican artifacts?

I am totally opposed to it. It's a very deep problem with thousands of little roots. But it's not something where you can cut the trunk and you've gotten rid of the problem. In this region, as long as there is poverty, people will always use the occasional find of something beautiful to get out of poverty. How can you say to a person, "No, don't sell that jade ax to save your child who's sick, who needs to go to the hospital and have an operation?"

I think education helps a lot. To constantly say, "You need to protect this. If you find something, give it to the museum, because people will come see the museum. And if people come, they will spend money, and that will economically help your town."

Here's a story: I built a tiny museum in another community. For many years, it had no electricity and a poor road. In this town, a quarter, 25 cents, is a fortune. After building the museum, I made friends with a couple of sisters. And I found out they knew how to make pottery. I said, "Hey, now you've got a museum, and people are going to come here. Let's make some interesting things out of pottery so you can sell them."

I spent my lunch breaks helping the girls. We were making cups like crazy! Then a group from Colorado asked me to take them on a tour, so I took them to the town. And I said, "Look, the girls are going to sell you pottery. If you don't like it, buy it anyway. It's only five pesos. To them, five pesos is a fortune."

The sisters had taken a little wooden table down to the museum and put all the cups on it and filled them with tropical flowers. These people from Colorado were the nicest people in the world. They saw these cute little girls, and they bought everything! And the girls were ecstatic.

Then one time when I wasn't there, another group of tourists came. They got off the bus and said, "Oh, that's just junk." The sisters were shattered, but I said to them, "This is a better activity. You can do it in your spare time at home, and it's legal. There's always going to be great people and not so great. The next group might buy everything."

I often think of the litterbug campaign in the United States. The roads and streets were full of garbage, and the litterbug campaign was a slow brainwash from one generation to the next. It's the same thing with looting. You've got to get to the kids. They're the future, and they're the ones who are going to say, "No, we don't loot, and we don't sell."

The roots of the problem are deep and massive. Sometimes I look at the museum we built [in San Lorenzo], and I think, well, it's a start. Then two days later I hear how somebody found a piece and sold it. It's up and down.

Looting doesn't promote any respect for the past. Once a piece is removed from the ground, it has no context. When a projectile point is in the ground, you can find out if it's next to a cooking area or in an area where the Olmec stored weapons or hunting equipment. The context gives you that extra piece of information that helps you understand the past. If you *don't* save the context, then you're losing a major part of the past.

If you could travel back to the Olmec civilization, what mystery would you most like to solve?
I wouldn't look for any particular mystery. I'd want to spend a great deal of time in a place like San Lorenzo and get to know everybody. I'd get into their houses and get to know their kids. Then I could understand how artifacts relate to society.

When I came back to the present, I'd see pottery vessels and say, "Oh, yes, of course. Those are what the Olmec used for cooking fish. Or those are what they used for cooking beans." And I'd go into the ruler's sacred precinct. Does he actually sit on his throne? Who's around him? I'd want to be there, nosier than heck, getting into everybody's lives. I'd probably follow them to the bathroom! The mystery of archaeology is seeing evidence and translating it into the human past. The space between the one and the other is the mystery of archaeology.

Continued from page 23

Achiote is a Nahuatl word for a tropical shrub. Mesoamericans stir their chocolate drink with the root to give it a pleasing musky flavor. They also use powdered achiote to add flavor and a yellow color to foods such as rice and stews.

Then a remarkable discovery surprised them all in May 1994. Spring temperatures in San Lorenzo soar over 100 degrees Fahrenheit, and high humidity keeps the air as steamy as a hot bath. On May 2, a local man was tramping through this sweltering countryside, searching for an **achiote** bush. He wandered into a deep ravine and came across an unusual rock. Excited, he reported his find to Cyphers.

The next day, she sent workers to investigate. They didn't find the rock, but they found something else nearby: a giant nose under a thin layer of soil. Above the nose, a small section of ancient eyeball calmly stared up, as if unimpressed by the 20th century. One of the workers ran to Cyphers with his astonishing news. "We found a colossal head, we *think*!" he proudly announced.

Olmec head, San Lorenzo, Mexico, 1200 BCE.

"This is not a good time for joking," Cyphers replied firmly. She never imagined the men would ever find a head, but it was true. The discovery was a setback in a way, because local people focused again on the heads and forgot about the lives of ordinary Olmec. Still, Cyphers remembers May 3, 1994, as the most exciting moment of her life as an archeologist.

Ann Cyphers is one of many scientists to uncover Olmec sculptures in the Gulf Coast area of Mexico. A geographer reported seeing a head in 1862, and a tourist spotted one in 1925. In 1940, the Smithsonian Institution and the National Geographic Society sent archaeologists Matthew and Marion Stirling to see the heads for themselves.

The Stirlings uncovered five more heads. Some were more than nine feet high. They also found a 40-ton throne

40-ton Olmec throne, Tabasco, Mexico, around 1200 BCE

carved with images of gods. It depicts a dead Olmec ancestor emerging from a cave, with his living relatives connected to him by a rope that symbolizes kinship. When Matthew Stirling reported the findings in *National Geographic Magazine* in 1941, thrilled readers got their first glimpse of a mysterious civilization called the Olmec.

Until that point, everyone believed that the Maya had built the first civilization in Mexico. However, Stirling was convinced that the heads were signs of a mother culture:

THE MAYA OF MESOAMERICA

The Maya culture was one of many that blossomed in ancient Mesoamerica. From 1000 BCE to the present, Maya people have lived in the eastern third of Mesoamerica. Ancient Maya cities flourished between 250 and 900 CE.

RADIOCARBON DATING

Every plant and animal on Earth contains the element radiocarbon. When something dies, its radiocarbon starts disappearing, but that takes a very long time. Only half of it is gone after 5,568 years. Half of what's left is gone after another 5,568 years. After about 50,000 years, all the radiocarbon finally disappears. Workers in a radiocarbon laboratory can estimate the age of a once-living object by measuring how much radiocarbon is left.

the source of all art styles and religious myths that trickled down to later Mesoamerican civilizations. Other archaeologists hotly disagreed! Who was Stirling to say that the Maya weren't as original as they had all thought?

The argument simmered until the late 1940s. It was solved when a chemist invented radiocarbon dating. This technology allows scientists to determine the precise age of a natural substance like charcoal. Archaeologists tested wood charcoal from ancient Olmec hearths. They found that it was 500 years older than charcoal from the earliest Maya sites. So, if the Olmec came before the Maya, they built the first civilization in Mesoamerica, right? Maybe not.

Archeologists love digging, especially when digs uncover more information. Digs in the 1970s proved that people in the Valley of Oaxaca carved pictures of gods on pottery long before the Olmec carved heads or thrones. Now many archaeologists think the Olmec was a sister culture—slightly younger than the Valley of Oaxaca, slightly older than the Maya, but growing around the same time.

Either way, colossal heads lead to colossal questions. The Olmec carved stone heads from a volcanic rock called basalt, but basalt is unavailable in San Lorenzo. The heads weigh as much as 17 tons, but ancient Mesoamerica had no beasts of burden. Where did the Olmec find basalt rocks? How did they move them? Whose heads did they carve into stone? And why did they go to all that trouble, anyway?

Ancient riverbeds around San Lorenzo hold some answers. The rivers flooded each year, leaving a gift of rich soil behind. Over time, this fertile soil mounded into high levees, or banks. Maize grew well on the levees, which held so much moisture that the lucky people who lived there could harvest two crops of maize in one growing season.

These families piled extra maize into canoes and set off down the rivers. By trading maize along the way, they became rich. The wealth meant they could hold feasts for their village, and who doesn't like a delicious meal? Feasts drew people to the community, and when the newcomers settled down, the village became a town.

In other words, a rich Olmec was a popular guy who threw great parties for guests who never went home. Such a man could easily win the confidence of people and call himself their leader.

As proof of power, these leaders must have ordered artists to carve their images in stone. Mountains were sacred places to ancient Mesoamericans. It makes sense, then, that an Olmec leader who thought highly of himself would want his image carved from sacred rock. A volcanic mountain range lies about 35 miles northwest of San Lorenzo. Some archaeologists think Olmec laborers traveled to these mountains to find huge chunks of basalt. Then they floated them to San Lorenzo on wooden rafts.

Ann Cyphers believes this is only partly true, because a raft would sink under the massive weight. She thinks the Olmec built sledges and hauled the mammoth stones over hills and through swamps to San Lorenzo. Then armies of laborers dragged the rocks up to the plateau and set them in place in a basalt workshop.

A total of 40 heads, thrones, and other sculptures have been found around the plateau. The monuments suggest

These jade statues found at La Venta, each about seven or eight inches high, were deliberately buried in a sacred place and probably represent a gathering of Olmec ancestors.

that, for a long while, San Lorenzo dominated the Olmec region. But something strange happened around 900 BCE. Someone chipped off pieces of the thrones and buried the heads. Then people abandoned the plateau. No one knows why.

Maybe another Olmec group invaded San Lorenzo. The Olmec settlement of La Venta is 50 miles northeast of the plateau. A leader of La Venta might have overrun San Lorenzo and forced the people out.

LIKE MONEY IN THE BANK

La Venta is on the coast of the Gulf of Mexico. People in this Olmec settlement grew lots of maize, but their leftover harvests quickly rotted in the warm, damp, tropical climate. To avoid losing that wealth, they traded maize for jade and other green stones. Then artists carved the stones into beautiful figurines. La Venta's crafts-people made carvings of such high quality that jade became a way of measuring riches in ancient Mesoamerica.

The leaders of La Venta deliberately buried dozens of these figurines. They also ordered workers to cut more than 1,000 tons of green serpentine, a stone similar to jade, into large flat bricks and bury them, too. The burials were the Olmec's way of repaying the gods for bringing precious rain. The people never touched these nest eggs. Raiders have robbed a few burial sites over the centuries, but the rest remained undisturbed until archaeologists excavated them in the 1950s.

Cyphers has another theory. She thinks volcanic eruptions in the nearby mountains may have changed the routes of the rivers. If so, that would have interrupted trade. With no way of trading extra maize, an Olmec leader would find himself a poor man with low status. Then tired laborers might have revolted against him.

We can only guess what happened. Meanwhile, more monuments, houses, and workshops wait patiently under the earth in the Land of Rubber. Curious archaeologists like Ann Cyphers will find and study them, bringing us closer to understanding the mysterious Olmec.

MAJOR GODS OF MESOAMERICA

REALM	AZTEC NAME	ENGLISH TRANSLATION
creation	Ometeotl	*Two God (Dual God)*
rain	Tlaloc	*Storm God*
sun	Tonatiuh	*Sun Disk*
wind	Ehecatl	*Wind*
fire	Xiuhtecuhtli	*God of Fire*
moon	Coyolxauhqui	*Warrior Maiden*
maize	Xilonen	*Young Maize*
night, war	Tezcatlipoca	*Smoking Mirror*
war, the sun	Huitzilopochtli	*Hummingbird on the Left*
games, music	Xochipilli	*Flower Lord*
death	Mictlantecuhtli	*God of Hell*

CHAPTER 3

CONQUESTS AND CAPTIVES

THE FIRST MESOAMERICAN CITIES

One Earthquake was a VIP—a Very Important Person. His stone portrait, engraved some time before 500 BCE in the Valley of Oaxaca, tells us he was probably the chief of a Zapotec village. He certainly looked the part.

When One Earthquake was only four days old, his parents strapped two boards tightly to the front and back of his head. Eventually, the painful pressure molded the top of his soft baby skull into a cone shape. Noble Zapotec families felt that this gave their sons a dignified air.

One Earthquake was a sharp dresser, too, thanks to a family in his village who polished iron into mirrors. He bartered something—extra maize, perhaps—for the mirrors. Then he traded the mirrors for jade earrings. Every time he wore the precious stones, he flaunted his position and wealth.

One Earthquake must have let the wealth go to his pointy head, because he got in trouble with the ruler of San José Mogote. This was the largest village in the Valley of Oaxaca, and One Earthquake should have left it alone. But for some reason, he angered San José Mogote's leader. Maybe One Earthquake wanted to farm fertile fields that surrounded the larger village. Or maybe the chief of San

WHAT'S IN A NAME?

Ancient Mesoamericans observed a sacred 260-day calendar. The calendar had a 13-day cycle similar to our cycle of a 7-day week. It also had a cycle of 20 signs such as Flower, Rabbit, Serpent, Death, and Earth Movement, or Earthquake (13 days × 20 signs = 260-day calendar).

Parents gave a child two names: one for the number of the day on which he or she was born, and one for the sign. One Earthquake was born on the first day of the 13-day cycle, on a day with the sign of Earthquake.

A 16th-century Aztec scribe penned these drawings on a codex (bark-paper book) to name places in the Valley of Oaxaca. From left to right the glyphs are Miahuapan (Canal of the Maize Tassels), Tototepec (Hill of the Bird), Ocelotepec (Hill of the Jaguar), and Cuicatlán (Place of Song).

José Mogote was hungry for One Earthquake's fields, and our hero decided he should fight back.

Most likely, One Earthquake went to San José Mogote with warriors, and San José Mogote's warriors overcame them. Then the captors stripped One Earthquake and removed his beating heart with an obsidian dagger. On a stone slab almost five feet tall, they carved an image of his death.

As a final insult, they added a hieroglyphic nametag between his legs so everyone would know the name of their

“ Stone portrait of One Earthquake's death, San José, Mexico, 500 BCE.

victim: the symbol by his heel means *one*, and the symbol just above means *earthquake*. When the chief of San José Mogote enlarged his temple, he set the slab in place as a doorsill. From then on, anyone who walked inside stepped on a picture of One Earthquake.

With no leader, the people of One Earthquake's village probably fell under the rule of San José Mogote. By 500 BCE, similar takeovers increased the population of San José Mogote to 2,000 people. Throughout these conquests, poor One Earthquake's portrait sent a gruesome message: if you mess with the big boys, we'll stomp on you.

The joining of these villages under one ruler was a small

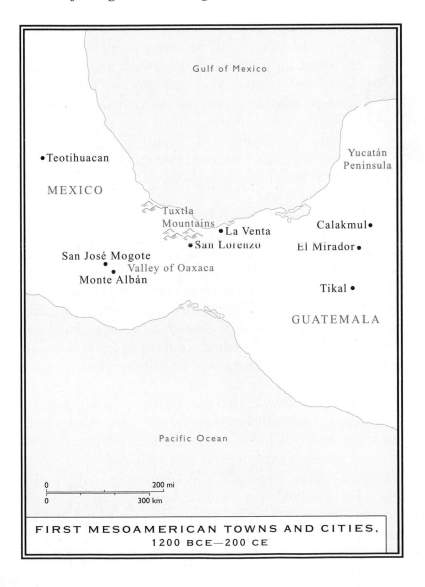

FIRST MESOAMERICAN TOWNS AND CITIES,
1200 BCE—200 CE

The high god of the Zapotec royal family, called Cocijo in Zapotec, was a local descendant of the god of lightning that was carved into earlier Mesoamerican pottery. On this burial urn, Cocijo carries a water jar, from which he poured the life-giving waters from the sky.

example of what came next. Around 500 BCE, the Zapotec abandoned all their villages and even the thriving town of San José Mogote. They moved to a mountain called Monte Albán.

Monte Albán had no water supply, and the Zapotec had to level the top before anyone could live there. Why would so many people leave their cozy huts for a mountain 1,300 feet above the valley floor? Cociyo, the rain god, is part of the answer. Like the Olmec of San Lorenzo, people in Oaxaca wanted to please their rain god, and they thought sacrificial blood would do the trick. The chiefs might have believed that sacrifices made on a sacred mountain would surely put a smile on Cociyo's frowning face.

But how could the chiefs make such a barren place livable? The answer lies in the Oaxaca Valley's shape. Then, as now, three arms of land formed the valley, with one chief ruling each one. Monte Albán, smack in the center of the valley, was neutral territory. The three chiefs could unite as one royal family without giving up their home turf. By tripling their power, they controlled enough laborers to build the city. Laborers dug out hundreds of terraces for houses and gardens. They also dug irrigation systems for crops growing at the base of the mountain.

The word *stucco* comes from an old German word for "crust." The Maya made stucco by burning limestone until it was powder. Then they blended the powder with water and coated the outside of their buildings with the mixture.

Other work crews leveled the mountaintop and paved it with **stucco**. They built a market and large reservoir for storing water during dry seasons. In a center plaza, they constructed palaces, a sunken patio, and a ball court for rubber-ball games. Most important, the laborers erected temples where leaders could offer sacrifices to the cranky Cociyo.

The Zapotec now called themselves the Cloud People. Archaeologists think that by 400 BCE, more than 5,000 Cloud People resided in the spectacular mountaintop city.

Two thousand more lived on terraces built into its slopes. Others lived in foothills that surround the peak.

As Monte Albán grew, it attracted a variety of new residents. Archaeologists have found mirrors, shell jewelry, feather headdresses, and pottery buried in the city's tombs. These valuables show that a population of artists with various skills moved from the surrounding countryside to Monte Albán. The city sounds like a great place for a craft fair, but it was much more.

By 200 CE, Monte Albán was a small kingdom with one ruler. More than 20,000 people in the valley and beyond lived under his thumb. The largest city of its day in the Americas had been born.

City life was safer than country life, because outside invaders could hardly rip out 20,000 beating hearts at once. Shopping was convenient, too. A resident could walk out of his hut, trade goods with a neighbor, and end up with a stash of cacao pods or a pair of dangling jade earrings. And more people made finding a husband or wife easier, too.

Monte Albán's rulers were powerful and aggressive. Archaeologists know this from 300 conquest slabs that leaders carved on the outside wall of the largest building in the city. Called *danzantes*, these carvings are portraits of enemies

danzantes (dahn-SAHN-tehs) = "dancers" in Spanish. The figures looked like dancers to Spaniards, who first saw the stones standing upright in 1519 CE.

This portrait of a bleeding warrior in the Valley of Oaxaca is accompanied by hieroglyphs on both sides of his head that give his name. Such figures are shown with their eyes closed and in contorted poses (leading to the nickname "danzantes," or "dancers"), leading archaeologists to deduce that they represent warriors killed in battle or sacrificed after the battle.

who resisted Monte Albán's control. Like One Earthquake, each nude figure lies in a twisted position. Later rulers simply carved the names of places they defeated in battle or won over peaceably. Canal of the Maize Tassels, Hill of the Bird, Hill of the Jaguar, Place of Song—all belonged to Monte Albán.

Around 900 CE, Monte Albán's population dwindled to a mere few thousand Cloud People. Other towns outside the Valley of Oaxaca were rising in power. Perhaps these places seemed more attractive to the Zapotec. Or maybe the kingdom became too big for one leader to control alone. Archaeologists don't know exactly why the great Monte Albán ended after 1,400 years. Meanwhile, another city was rising out of tropical rainforests to the east.

Between 350 and 200 BCE, the Maya built one of their first cities east of the Valley of Oaxaca. Eighty miles of dense, dripping forests surround **El Mirador** in all directions, making the ground underneath soggy. How could the Maya turn these swamps into usable farmland for growing maize? Terraced fields were out of the question, because the land was flat. The Maya solution was to clear trees first. Then they made raised fields by scooping up earth from the bottom of the swamp. This icky stuff was rich with fish excrement and rotted organic matter, so crops thrived in it. Converting swamps into farms was a messy job, but it was worth the trouble. It meant the Maya could grow bumper crops of maize, beans, and squash.

In Oaxaca and throughout the Maya realm, people added meat to their diet by attracting deer to their fields and yards. The Maya in El Mirador also found meat simply by looking up. Rainforests in eastern Mesoamerica are a thick canopy of cedar, mahogany, and gum trees. Amazing animals live at different heights within the leafy umbrella: howler monkeys whose guttural howls slice through the mist, macaws, lizards, and frogs. All of them were tasty to the ancient Maya. The people of El Mirador maintained different canopy levels around the city by clearing certain trees. The animals felt at home, and the rainforest became a kind of McMonkey's for fast, easy food.

el mirador (el meer-ah-DOR) = "the lookout point" in Spanish. Local workers who first discovered the ancient city were climbing tall gum trees. They looked out and saw the tops of pyramids rising above the forest.

Once the Maya solved the food problem, they could attract the immense number of workers needed for building a city. Hundreds of elaborate buildings coated with stucco prove that the Maya were expert architects. The Tigre Pyramid, one of three in the city, is 180 feet high. With a base the size of three football fields, it's one of the largest buildings ever constructed by the ancient Maya.

Accomplished engineers, the Maya also built raised roads that were higher than the level of water in the swamp. These allowed trade with smaller towns in the rainforest. One of the roads was 13 feet high and 25 miles long—all of it built by hand, because no beasts of burden lived in ancient Mesoamerica.

The Maya were gifted artists, too. Archaeologists have found giant sculptures carved on the stucco walls of El

An overall view of El Mirador shows the massive Danta Complex towering above the jungle. The red paint on the temple pyramids in El Mirador signified the sun rising in the east.

Stairway, Tigre Complex, El Mirador, 2nd century BCE

FROM MAIZE TO MINES

5000 BCE
Farmers grow maize in the Valley of Oaxaca

1400–850 BCE
Farmers in Oaxaca use pot irrigation

1350–850 BCE
One-room houses are common in Oaxaca

1200–500 BCE
Olmec people mine basalt for making colossal heads

500 BCE
Zapotec build Monte Albán

350 BCE
Maya mine limestone for making stucco buildings in El Mirador

900 CE
Monte Albán falls

Mirador's buildings. One is an earth god shown as a jaguar. Another is a rain god, a cousin of the Olmec's Sky Dragon and the Zapotec's Cociyo.

El Mirador is so remote that few archaeologists travel there. Since local workers discovered it in 1926, only eight teams have made the journey. Despite their research, we still know little about the city. How many people lived in El Mirador? Did they have a variety of skills, like the residents of Monte Albán? Why did they leave?

The people of El Mirador would have burned constant fires to make limestone powder for their stucco buildings. One archaeologist thinks they cleared too many trees for the fires. Massive erosion would then have washed soil into the swamps and ruined the raised fields. In other words, no maize, no people, no city.

Or perhaps El Mirador was warring with its neighbors. So far, archaeologists haven't found conquest slabs or *danzantes* like those in Monte Alban. Do the stones lie under a tangle of jungle vines? Possibly, but no one has found them yet. This earliest of all Mayan cities requires time, money, and more bold archaeologists before we learn definite answers. For now, most of El Mirador's secrets remain shrouded in forests and mist.

CHAPTER 4

PYRAMIDS, PAINTINGS, AND POTTERY

TEOTIHUACAN, CITY OF THE GODS

❝ A SCULPTURE OF FEATHERED SERPENT AND A MURAL FROM TEOTIHUACAN

Tourists who visit a big city are often easy to spot, because they like looking up at the tall buildings. Ancient Mesoamerican sightseers weren't exactly tourists. They were more like pilgrims who traveled to sacred cities and paid their respects. But when they visited **Teotihuacan**, in central Mexico, they must have done what any tourist today would do: look up. That's because Teotihuacan has the highest pyramids ever built in Mesoamerica.

Archaeologists aren't sure if one group of people such as the Zapotec built the city, or if a mix of various groups built it. They only know that construction started around the year 100 CE. For unknown reasons, much of Teotihuacan burned around 600 CE.

In the 1960s, archaeologists began mapping the site of the long-deserted city. First, they marked off the area in 500-meter, or 1/4-mile, squares. Within each square, they looked for pottery fragments, pieces of shell, and obsidian flakes lying on the ground. In the 1970s, archaeologists prepared a drawing of the city, its monuments, and outlying neighborhoods. Teotihuacan covered 16 square miles and was the largest Mesoamerican city of its day.

"teo" + "tihuacan" = "gods" + "the place of" in Nahuatl. We don't know the original name of the city. Six hundred years after invaders burned the temples, the Aztecs named it Teotihuacan, or city of the gods.

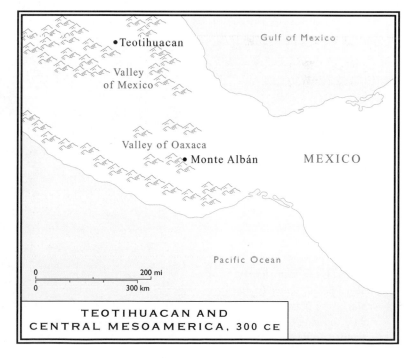

Teotihuacan

Gulf of Mexico

Valley of Mexico

Valley of Oaxaca

• Monte Albán

MEXICO

Pacific Ocean

0   200 mi
0   300 km

TEOTIHUACAN AND CENTRAL MESOAMERICA, 300 CE

But why was it built? Archaeologists think volcanoes provide the answer.

In 50 BCE, a volcano in the southern part of the Valley of Mexico blew its top. Fifty years later, a second volcano called Smoking Mountain exploded. The lava and hot fiery ash destroyed every village within thirty miles. Fearful of a third explosion, the people fled to a hot desert area in the northern part of the valley. They stopped running when they reached Fat Mountain.

Here was the ideal spot for a brand new city. When the refugees saw springs flowing from Fat Mountain's slopes, they built a reservoir and saved the water.

The San Juan River was another bonanza. People figured they could dig ditches and channel the river directly into fields with the best soil. They were right. As soon as they harvested one crop from the well-watered fields, they planted another. Year-round crops fed a growing population, and by 400 CE, 125,000 people called the city home.

While mapping Teotihuacan, archaeologists found more than 2,000 group dwellings that they call apartment compounds. Made of adobe coated with concrete, each

A painted mural from the apartment compound of Tepantitla in Teotihuacan reveals a Meso-american version of paradise. The mountain of abundance in the center provides water for irrigated fields, while happy, well-fed people dance (right center), sing (figure at lower right), and play three kinds of ballgames (top left).

was the size of one city block and contained three or four apartments. These were further divided into four or five rooms. The windowless rooms were dark and cool, while outside courtyards and porches provided sunshine and fresh air.

These comfortable lodgings were a big improvement over the one-room thatched huts that most Mesoamericans lived in. Perhaps this is why thousands of artists moved to the city. Thousands more were trained in local schools. You probably like decorating your bedroom with brightly colored pictures. Artists in Teotihuacan felt the same way about their apartment walls. Using shades of red, green, blue, and yellow, they painted lively scenes of gods, goddesses, and life in their beloved city.

Hieroglyphic writing on some of the murals identifies deities, including a goddess with painted fingernails. The Storm God, a relative of other Mesoamerican water gods, wears a tasseled headdress and shell goggles. Archaeologists aren't sure what these mysterious eyepieces mean. But they do know that pictures of the Storm God show him wearing goggles in place of eyes. And if a warrior is in the service of

the Storm God, he is pictured wearing round goggles with eyes inside the circles.

Another mural shows springs pouring from Fat Hill and canals channeling water into fields. Hieroglyphic writing identifies Wooded Hill and Flowery Hill—smaller peaks where plants are nourished by the springs of Fat Hill.

Horizontal lines above Fat Hill represent a ball court. Between the lines, two men are playing with a rubber ball. Happy swimmers cool off in the mountain springs, and a gleeful man rides piggyback. Sound scrolls curling from their mouths express joy at living in this earthly paradise. No wonder pilgrims liked to visit Teotihuacan—they knew they would have a fantastic time!

You can take in the sights of the city through the eyes of a hypothetical pilgrim. Let's say the year is 300 CE. And let's say he's walked 400 miles from Monte Albán, a mountain-top city in the Valley of Oaxaca.

The city planners built the majestic **Moon Pyramid** first, so the pilgrim might start his tour there. Always grateful for water, city builders placed a statue of the Goddess of

Scholars don't know the original name of the Moon Pyramid. Like the Sun Pyramid, it was named by the Aztecs 600 years after Teotihuacan burned.

A bird's eye view of the Street of the Dead, which is about 130 feet wide and 3 miles long. Hundreds of thousands of pilgrims and traders walked the avenue in ancient times to worship at the great temples and trade in the city's markets. Centuries later, the Aztecs named it "The Street of the Dead" because they believed that the rulers of the aban-doned city were buried in the temples that lined this great road.

Standing Water at the base of the pyramid. She honors the life-giving springs of Fat Hill, so the pilgrim leaves an offering for her—some tortillas, perhaps, or a live turkey. Then he climbs the pyramid for an eagle's eye view.

The broad Avenue of the Dead stretches south for more than two miles. Temples and palaces line the long corridor; bodies of previous leaders are buried deep within each one. Looking to the left, our traveler sees the gigantic Sun Pyramid. He might very well gasp at the sight, because the terraced pyramid matches exactly the shape of a mountain behind it. A secret tunnel dedicated to the Storm God lies under this pyramid. Our pilgrim would dearly love to see the tunnel and leave burnt offerings there, but only priests and the wealthiest people are allowed inside.

Now our traveler clambers down the steps of the Moon Pyramid. He strolls along the wide avenue, past the Sun Pyramid. Then he comes upon immense walls surrounding a temple called the Citadel. He may already know that the temple is dedicated to the Feathered Serpent god. In case he forgets, ferocious serpent heads made of stone jut from all sides of the building. The jaws seem to snap at him as he hurries by, reminding him to show some respect. The pilgrim also may have heard that when city planners built the Citadel, they sacrificed 200 warriors and buried them inside. The thought would not be too upsetting. Back home in Monte Albán, he has seen stone carvings of sacrificed victims. He believes that such deaths are occasionally necessary, because people must feed the gods, just as the gods feed them.

" Sculpture of Feathered Serpent, Teotihuacan

When our hypothetical pilgrim crosses the street and steps inside the Great Compound, a deafening pandemoni-

HUNGRY GODS

Ancient Mesoamericans usually left offerings of food for the gods: tortillas, gruel made from maize, and an occasional turkey. Bloodletting was only for special occasions such as the dedication of a temple. Offerings and sacrifices repaid the gods for sending rain and sunshine—the life-giving forces necessary for crops to grow.

Felines were very popular in the murals and sculptures of Teotihuacan, with jaguar sculptures adorning many of the principal temples, including the Pyramid of the Sun. Carved from onyx, this jaguar has a receptacle on its back for receiving offerings.

um greets him. Traders from the Gulf Coast are selling jade ornaments, jaguar pelts, parrot and quetzal feathers, and rubber balls by the dozens. Traders from the Pacific Coast jostle among the crowd, hawking jewelry they've carved from seashells.

The pilgrim is impressed with the variety of crafts sold by Teotihuacan's traders: obsidian blades shaped like people, stone bowls and sculptures, and thousands of ceramic figurines made of fired clay. He eyes a charming obsidian blade that's only two inches long. When he left home, he brought a piece of shimmering mineral called mica with him—should he trade one for the other? Yes! The blade will bring him much prestige and a good price back in the Valley of Oaxaca.

Suppose our pilgrim wants to see where artists make these items. When he leaves the Great Compound, he crosses the avenue, wanders behind the Citadel, and enters a pottery workshop. The sight inside is astounding. Our man from Oaxaca has often seen women at home shaping pottery by hand. But the number of artists working here amazes him. Hundreds of women with nimble fingers are molding vessels with little clay feet. Others are making clay masks shaped like butterflies, bird heads, flowers, and seashells.

Small figurines from 5 to 20 inches tall are the most appealing of all. When the pilgrim picks up a completed figure, he notices a small door in its chest. Puzzled, he gently opens it, and finds six miniature clay people inside—one in each arm and leg, one in the head, and one in the chest. If asked, the potter might say they are members of an important local family.

The pottery workshop was exciting, but like most travelers, our tourist is probably tired after hours of walking. He crosses the avenue again and heads for the ball courts. These are marked off by stones and located in an open area south of the Great Compound. What a relief! For a few hours, he can rest his feet while he watches a rubber-ball game.

Our invented pilgrim is stuck in 300 CE, unaware of the influence Teotihuacan will have on the rest of Mesoamerica. But thanks to archaeologists, we know what happened. In the faraway Maya area, they've found hieroglyphic texts about this splendid city. The glyphs discuss trips the Maya made to the city of the gods, and trips that people from Teotihuacan made to the Maya realm.

Archaeologists have also unearthed Teotihuacan crafts in dozens of Maya settlements. One Maya pot shows people leaving a Teotihuacan temple and arriving at a Maya temple. Objects like these show that Teotihuacan traded with Maya who lived 900 long miles away. The Maya even copied the architecture of Teotihuacan's pyramids. The city set trends and styles, just as Rome, San Francisco, New York, and Tokyo do today.

Shortly after 550 CE, vandals burned small temples that sat on top of the Sun and Moon pyramids. They also destroyed temples lining the Avenue of the Dead. Did residents rebel against the government? Some archaeologists say yes, because only temples were torched, and people kept on living in many of the apartment compounds. Other archaeologists think resentful outsiders destroyed only the temples because these were symbols of the city's great power.

Either way, Teotihuacan has lived on in memory for more than 1,400 years. On the first day of spring every year, a million tourists climb the Sun Pyramid. From the top, they celebrate the spring equinox, when the sun is in the sky for exactly 12 hours. They can also remember the city's great contributions to art and religion.

Like the European city of Rome, Teotihuacan was—and still is—the "eternal city" of Mesoamerica.

FRAGMENTS, FINGERPRINTS, AND THE FBI

The ground at Teotihuacan is still covered with thousands of figurine fragments. In 1975, archaeologist Warren Barbour noticed a curious thing about them: the makers had left fingerprints on the damp clay, and all the prints swirled to the left. Barbour asked the Federal Bureau of Investigation, the world's greatest experts on fingerprints, about this odd uniformity. The answer was simple. Male fingerprints always swirl to the right, and female fingerprints always swirl to the left.

Barbour wasn't too surprised. He already knew from written native history that Mesoamerican women made pottery. Still, the FBI's reply gave him hard evidence: women had produced the millions of ceramic figurines in Teotihuacan. They were key to the city's success as a great center of trade.

CHAPTER 5

K'UK' MO' TAKES A HIKE
WRITTEN HISTORY TAKES A LEAP

" INSCRIPTIONS ON
A MAYA ALTAR,
A STELA, AND
POPOL VUH

"quetzal macaw lord"
in Mayan }

" Inscriptions on Altar Q,
Copán, Honduras, 763 CE

Teotihuacan was one of the great capital cities of ancient Mesoamerica. It was also a place where men became kings. Sometime in 426 CE, a Maya noble named **K'uk' Mo' Ajaw** may have traveled 900 miles to Teotihuacan for just this reason.

Scholars aren't sure where K'uk' Mo' started his trip. Some believe he came from Copán in present-day Honduras. That's because 300 years later, Maya artists carved a huge table-altar in Copán that tells about K'uk' Mo's hike and kingship. Called Altar Q, the stone is 4½ feet long on

each side and 27 inches high. The sides are carved with 17 sculptures of seated men, including K'uk' Mo'.

On the top, scribes—people who write—carved 36 hieroglyphs. These carvings are more than nametags that label a person or place—they're signs standing for syllables and words. Written in complete thoughts, they're one of the earliest Mesoamerican examples of true writing. But the carvings don't tell all of K'uk' Mo's story.

To fill in the gaps, archaeologists have excavated 160 ancient buildings in Copán. K'uk' Mo' built many of them. Archaeologists have also found eight more portraits of K'uk' Mo'. And in 1995, they uncovered his brittle bones in a dark, dusty tomb.

More work remains. The Hieroglyphic Stairway in Copán is made of stones carved with 2,200 glyphs. The longest text in ancient America, the stairway tells the city's history, starting with K'uk' Mo'. Perhaps when **epigraphers** have translated all the glyphs, they'll understand the complete history of K'uk' Mo'. What they know so far is this:

Glyphs on Altar Q say that someone named K'uk' Mo' Ajaw sat in a place called the *wi'te'naab*, or Tree Root House. The inscriptions don't reveal the location of this mysterious place, but many archaeologists think it was Teotihuacan. The glyphs don't say what happened in the Tree Root House, either. Perhaps K'uk' Mo' was already a king but needed approval from priests in Teotihuacan. Or maybe priests there actually named him king. Whatever the reason, K'uk' Mo' underwent some sort of ritual.

The next glyph is a date telling us that three days went by. Then the inscriptions show a name change. The word *ajaw*, or lord, was dropped from the end. And the words *K'inich Yax*, or Great Sun Blue-Green, were added to the beginning. So, *K'uk' Mo' Ajaw*—Quetzal Macaw Lord—became *K'inich Yax K'uk' Mo'*—Great Sun Blue-Green Quetzal Macaw. From lord to great sun—this was quite a promotion!

K'uk' Mo's carved portrait on **Altar Q** shows he was given special goggles made of cut shell. These were the sign of a warrior who served the Storm God of Teotihuacan. On his right arm, K'uk' Mo' wore a shield decorated with a pic-

epi + *graphia* = "upon" + "writing," from ancient Greek. An epigrapher is someone who studies ancient writing on stone, pottery, and other objects.

Altar Q, Copán, Honduras, 763 CE

Altar Q was named by Alfred Maudslay, an English archaeologist who worked in Copán from 1884 to 1886. When he found a complete altar or stela, he named it with a letter from the alphabet. If the altar or stela was broken, he named it with a number.

HAVE A GOOD DAY!

Ancient Mesoamericans reckoned time using what archaeologists call a Long Count calendar. One day was a *k'in*. One month was a *winal*, or 20 *k'ins*. A *tun* was 18 *winals*, or 360 days (close to our year). A *bak'-tun* was 10 *k'atuns*—144,000 days, or about 400 years.

Mesoamerican calendars also included a solar calendar of 365 days, a lunar calendar important in agriculture, a Venus calendar consulted for picking dates for battles, a Mars calendar, an 819-day calendar that archaeologists don't understand, and a sacred calendar of 260 days.

Each day and year of these calendars had a number and name with a special meaning. Mesoamerican priests used all the calendars to make predictions about a particular day. But the many calendars could contradict one another. The question, "What kind of day will it be?" would have taken a very long time to answer in ancient Mesoamerica.

ture of the War Serpent, another Teotihuacan god. K'uk' Mo' may also have carried an image of a snake-footed god, the royal ancestor of Teotihuacan's kings. All the accessories announced that he was no longer an ordinary man—he was now half-god.

Ready to rule, K'uk' Mo' left the city of the gods for the trip home. The difficult journey would have led him over mountain passes, through swamps and jungles, and deep into hostile enemy territory. At times, the trip must have seemed endless.

But the dream of being king would have kept K'uk' Mo' walking, day after day—according to a date glyph carved on Altar Q, 153 days in all. Five months after leaving Teotihuacan, the weary ruler finally reached home. The next glyph on Altar Q stands for *hi-li-oke*, or "leg-resting" in the Mayan language. This means that K'uk' Mo' could finally rest his aching muscles when he reached "three mountain place," the ancient name for Copán. And who can blame him, after so much hiking? Then he went on to fulfill his destiny.

Archaeologists suspect that K'uk' Mo' had to face rival chiefs on his return. If fighting was necessary, he probably felt that the gods of Teotihuacan would protect him. Plus, an examination of his skeleton shows a broken right arm that never healed properly. At some point in his life, K'uk' Mo' became a leftie. If he fought the chiefs after breaking his right arm, he would have held a thrusting spear in his left hand. The unexpected angle might have served him well in battle.

But maybe fighting wasn't necessary. Maybe K'uk' Mo's fancy new name impressed his rivals and he took the throne with no resistance. As ruler, he would have needed to earn the loyalty of his subjects. He ordered work crews to build a temple in the style of Teotihuacan pyramids, which probably impressed them. And the ceremonial ball court his men built may have been a big hit, too.

K'uk' Mo' would have known that if he married the daughter of a Copán chieftain, at least one local family would support his rule. If that wife produced a son, K'uk'

Mo' could pass on his kingship. Then that son could pass the power to *his* son, and so on down through the centuries. It could be the start of a great dynasty of rulers.

K'uk' Mo' did find himself a wife, and they produced a son named Learned One. As K'uk' Mo' hoped, Learned One ruled next. In honor of his father, the son erected a stela, or

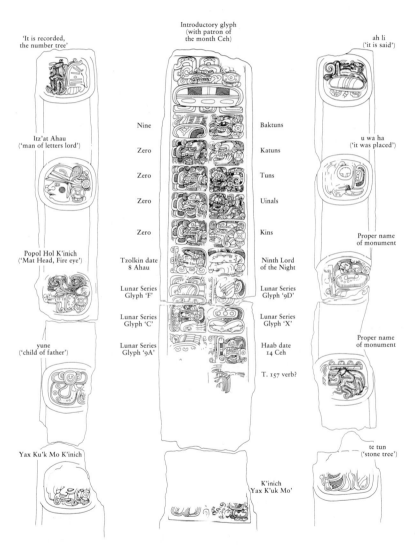

‘It is recorded, the number tree’

Itz'at Ahau ('man of letters lord')

Popol Hol K'inich ('Mat Head, Fire eye')

yune ('child of father')

Yax Ku'k Mo K'inich

Introductory glyph (with patron of the month Ceh)

Nine — Baktuns
Zero — Katuns
Zero — Tuns
Zero — Uinals
Zero — Kins
Tzolkin date 8 Ahau — Ninth Lord of the Night
Lunar Series Glyph 'F' — Lunar Series Glyph '9D'
Lunar Series Glyph 'C' — Lunar Series Glyph 'X'
Lunar Series Glyph '9A' — Haab date 14 Ceh
— T. 157 verb?

K'inich Yax K'uk Mo'

ah li ('it is said')

u wa ha ('it was placed')

Proper name of monument

Proper name of monument

te tun ('stone tree')

Stela 63, Copán, 435 CE

HIEROGLYPHS FOR DUMMIES

For almost 200 years, scholars have been unlocking the meanings of hieroglyphs, and the work continues. So far, they know that hieroglyphs are signs for words or syllables. Types of glyphs include:

date—when something happened

subject—who completed the action

verb—what happened, such as gave birth, married, rose to power, made war, got captured, or died

title—title of a person such as a lord or king

name—proper name of a person

emblem—name of the town where the person is from

upright stone. Then he carved it with both their names. The stela was Learned One's way of saying that his father was a great ruler, so he would be one, too.

Glyphs on the top of Altar Q tell the story of a trip made by K'inich Yax K'uk' Mo', the first king, to a great kingdom where he obtained the insignia of kingship. The story skips forward 340 years to the time when the city's last ruler had Altar Q carved in honor of K'inich and all the later kings of Copán. The dates on the altar show bars and dots for numerals in the solar and ritual calendar. The name of K'inich Yax K'uk' Mo' appears in the second column from the left, fifth glyph from the top.

HOW TO TELL A STONE STORY

Altar Q took teamwork. Archaeologists think that a crew of laborers must have first put the rock in place. Then a stonemason would have smoothed the surface. Then a painter would have drawn a grid of squares on top of the altar, then a glyph inside each square.

Following the painted lines, scribes engraved the hieroglyphs with stone chisels and wooden mallets. Then they smoothed away rough spots, leaving raised images with astonishing detail. Finally, one or more sculptors chiseled the intricate figures on the altar's sides.

The dynasty continued when one of Learned One's sons became king. Sixteen kings in all—the 17th ruled after the dynasty ended—governed Copán over the next four centuries. Each king increased Copán's wealth and power. By the end of the 600s CE, it was more than a mere city. It was a state controlling lands and people in valleys 70 miles away.

The kings of Copán never forgot who started their dynasty. In 763 CE, the last one placed the two-ton stone—Altar Q—in front of K'uk' Mo's tomb. Then the ruler's scribes and artists set to work. Through glyphs and sculptures, they recorded the history of K'uk' Mo's dynasty. And the story, as we know it so far, was complete.

How archaeologists discovered this much about K'uk' Mo' is a story itself. For a long while, modern researchers had no idea what the carvings or sculptures on Altar Q meant. Did the glyphs on top explain the figures on the side? Who were those men, anyway, with their crossed legs and feathered headdresses?

In 1912, one scholar thought the sculptures were astronomers discussing the stars. His theory stood for more than sixty years. In the 1970s, archaeologists figured out that the sculptures were portraits of kings sitting in order of their rule. And in the 1980s, they realized that each king was sitting on his name glyph. Some of the carved names are worn away. But the remaining ones have the ring of poetry, such as The Sky is Newly Revealed, Eighteen Are the Images of God, and Fire is the Mouth of the Snake.

But archaeologists were still stumped. The first figure sat on a name glyph that simply said "lord." Was he the first king of Copán? Epigrapher David Stuart began solving the puzzle in 1985.

Stuart already knew that ancient Mesoamericans name-tagged everything in sight with a glyph. In Monte Albán, the glyph for Place of Song meant a place where birds sang. In Teotihuacan, the Flowery Hill glyph meant a hill with flowers. Then Stuart noticed something odd about Maya nametags: glyphs painted on pots didn't always identify the pot as a pot. Instead, some glyphs named the pot's owner, as in, "This is the chocolate pot of Mr. So and So."

Stuart realized that the Maya had labeled Altar Q the same way. One of the 36 glyphs on top states, "This is the stone of K'inich Yax K'uk' Mo'." Was this fellow K'uk' Mo' the unidentified "lord" on the side of the altar?

Archaeologists guessed that the figure was an important person—maybe even the founder of the dynasty. Still, no one could prove it, until Stuart suddenly saw the mystery man's headdress in a new way. He noticed a quetzal feather, a macaw head, a sun glyph, and the glyph for green: the four parts of the name, K'inich Yax K'uk' Mo'.

One last discovery connected the carved clues. Archae-ologists found a man's skeleton buried at the bottom of the temple behind Altar Q. A jade pendant lay on the chest bone, and nearby were oyster shells carved with a royal title used by K'inich Yax K'uk' Mo'. Archaeologists had their man: K'uk' Mo' was the founder of the dynasty of kings carved on the sides of Altar Q.

Altar Q is a magnificent example of how the Maya wrote on stone. But they also recorded their history in thousands of paper books they made from deerskin or fig-tree bark. Some of the books are calendars in which Maya priests kept track of the movement of stars and planets. Astronomy was important to the Maya, because they believed these heaven-ly bodies were related to gods who controlled events on

MAYA MATH

In Maya mathematics, a bar stood for the number 5, and a dot represented the number 1. So, 6 was 1 bar and 1 dot, 17 was 3 bars and 2 dots. The Maya counted in base 20, rather than base 10, as we do. For 20, they used a shell sign with a dot over it. The shell sign basically acts as a placeholder, like zero in our system. With it, the Maya could write numbers in the millions, stacking collections of bars and dots vertically, which helped them to predict solar eclipses and movements of the planets over great spans of time. The Maya "zero" is one of the great achievements of the Mesoamerican mathemati-cians, not accomplished by the ancient Egyptians, Mesopotamians, or Greeks.

Earth. So, when a star or planet repeated its journey through the sky, history repeated itself below.

The planet Venus is a good example. Every year, this evening star disappears from the night sky and reappears a few months later. The Maya anxiously waited for Venus to return, because they believed this was the luckiest time for war. Many stone monuments record Maya night raids and battles that took place when Venus once again blinked out of the darkness.

popol + *vuh* = "community" + "book," "The Book of the Community" in Mayan

66 *Popol Vuh*, 1702 CE, copied from a more ancient manuscript

The **Popol Vuh** is a Maya book that describes how the gods created the world and people. It's also a book of genealogy, or family history, that traces the line of one royal Maya family: "After they had left there, they came here to the town. . . . There [began] the fifth generation of men, since the beginning of civilization and of the population, the beginning of the existence of the nation. There, then, they built many houses and at the same time constructed the Temple of God; in the center of the high part of the town they located it when they arrived and settled there."

In the top panel of a page from the Dresden Codex, an ear of corn is offered on a small stepped altar to honor the maize god. Maya priests observed solar, lunar, and planetary cycles and ensured that the ritual was done on the proper date in order to honor the maize god at the time of planting.

Mesoamericans were the only ancient people in the Americas who invented a system of writing and books. The Maya produced more writing than other Mesoamericans, and those in Copán produced the most glyphs of all. Without their inscribed stones and paper books, the written history of Mesoamerica would be a short one, indeed.

CHAPTER 6

THE BOY-KING OF BONE
AN EXPLOSION OF MAYA HIEROGLYPHS

" EMBLEM GLYPHS, HIEROGLYPHIC STAIRWAY, TEMPLE OF INSCRIPTIONS, BISHOP DIEGO DE LANDA, AND FRAY BERNARDINO DE SAHAGÚN

" Hieroglyphic stairway, Mexico, 647 CE

" Glyph, Temple of Inscriptions, 673 CE

The emblem glyph was gone. And the Maya kingdom of Bone—known today as Palenque—wanted it back. This desperate situation began in 599 CE, when Bone waged a battle with the rival kingdom of Calakmul. Archaeologists working in Bone have found a hieroglyphic stairway built in 647 CE. Glyphs, or carved signs, on the stairway hint at what happened during the battle.

There was an "axing" in Bone, the glyphs say, and sculptures of its gods were "thrown down." Archaeologists have

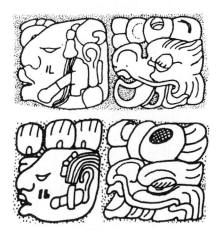

found more glyphs in the Temple of Inscriptions, built in 673 CE. The glyphs reveal that in 611, Calakmul attacked again. This time, Scroll Serpent, the king of Calakmul himself, led the battle. And again, Bone "was axed." Now two-time losers, the people of Bone could no longer carve the emblem for their kingdom: a screaming heron bird with feathers in its beak.

Instead, conquering warriors erected their own limestone monument in the heart of Bone. On the monument, they engraved a glyph that stood for *their* city's name. Like a flag planted on a battlefield, the glyph announced that Bone belonged to Calakmul.

Disaster struck the following year when the king of Bone died without naming a successor. Only his daughter, **Lady Sak K'uk'**, was left to rule the city. That was a

{ *Sak K'uk'* = "Resplendent Quetzal" in Mayan

problem, because the Maya believed that only kings could pass on leadership.

Scholars are still trying to figure out what happened next. They've found glyphs in Bone that say *no* rituals were performed during this time. Though her father wasn't alive to crown her, did Lady Sak K'uk' decide to make herself queen, anyway? However it happened, glyphs in the Temple of Inscriptions state that Lady Sak K'uk' became the ruler of Bone in 612 CE.

Temple of Inscriptions, Mexico, 673 CE

Lady Sak K'uk's reign lasted for three years. Glyphs in the Temple of Inscriptions that record this time are sorrowful. "Lost is the divine lady," they say, "lost is the lord."

Scholars don't know what this inscription means, but they think these three years were a period of great chaos. Maybe the people didn't want a self-appointed queen. Or maybe they thought only a man could lead warriors into battle and make Bone an independent kingdom again.

What to do, what to do? Lady Sak K'uk's husband couldn't rule. He was brave enough, and he came from a noble clan. But he wasn't descended from a royal family like Lady Sak K'uk'. There was only one answer: their son, **Pakal**, must be king. It was an unusual solution, because only kings, not queens, could name the next ruler. Besides, 12-year-old Pakal was young for such responsibility.

"shield" in Mayan }

Still, he would have been well educated by this time. Like all boys from noble Maya families, Pakal probably attended school. In the 16th century, a Spaniard named Diego de Landa described subjects that Maya children were learning in school at the time of the Spanish conquest. Topics included reading and writing hieroglyphs, "the computation of the years, months, and days, the festivals and ceremonies . . . the fateful days and seasons, their methods of [making] prophecies."

Bishop Diego de Landa, *The Account of the Things of Yucatan*, 16th century

And in the 16th century, a Spaniard named Bernardino de Sahagún mentions Aztec schools in his colonial chronicle, the *Florentine Codex*. Priests "corrected, and instructed" an Aztec boy, Sahagún wrote, so that "he might live an upright life." If Pakal was raised the same way as Aztec children, he was an obedient boy who would follow direc-

Fray Bernardino de Sahagún, *Florentine Codex*, 16th century

tions. His parents must have believed he could rule if he had some help.

And so, on July 29, 615 CE, the queen of Bone crowned her son. What child could forget such a moment? He remembered it so well that 32 years later he told an artist exactly how to carve the scene on a limestone slab. The slab shows that Lady Sak K'uk' prepared for the ceremony by putting on jewelry, a fancy woven shawl, and a matching skirt. Pakal wore a priceless jade pendant around his neck and arranged water lilies in his hair—a sign that he would govern a city blessed with rivers, streams, and waterfalls.

The boy took a seat on a jaguar-shaped throne reserved for kings. Then his mother placed a royal crown of quetzal feathers and jade beads on his young head. Pakal was now **K'inich Janaab' Pakal I**. With his parents' advice, he governed Bone and grew in strength and wisdom. Eventually, he defeated the rival city of Calakmul and captured some of their warriors. And finally the people of Bone could proudly carve their emblem glyph again.

{ "Great Sun Shield" in Mayan

After crowning her son, Lady Sak K'uk' lived another 25 years. Scholars are not quite sure what she was up to during this time, because there aren't any glyphs telling about her later years. The epigrapher Linda Schele thought she might have been worried about her father's relatives—that they would have considered Pakal a fake king because he inherited the throne from a woman.

After Pakal married at 23, he and his wife had two sons. The births were joyful events, but they must have caused more headaches for Lady Sak K'uk'. What would happen after Pakal died? Would the people question either of her grandsons' right to rule?

A hieroglyphic text inside the Temple of the Inscriptions at Palenque tells the life story of King Janaab' Pakal I. At the end of the king's long life, he was buried in a tomb beneath the stairway of the temple-pyramid.

In 1990, Linda Schele carefully studied the emblem glyph for Bone. She noticed that it was similar to the one for Lady Sak K'uk' in the Temple of Inscriptions. And those two glyphs looked very much like the one for First Mother, the goddess who created Bone's three main gods. To Schele, the glyphs suggested how Grandmamma Sak K'uk' could have kept kingship in the family.

All Maya rulers became gods or goddesses after death. When Lady Sak K'uk' died, Pakal had to convince people she was no run-of-the-mill goddess. She was the First Mother. And because her grandsons were related to a deity, they should inherit kingship. Pakal had a tough job ahead of him. How could he turn Lady Sak K'uk' into the goddess of creation? Talk was cheap. Only writing—glyphs carved in ageless stone—could make it official.

After his mother's death, Pakal would construct new buildings. Then laborers would carry huge limestone slabs inside and place them against the walls. On the slabs, scribes would etch glyphs tracing Pakal's kinship back to the First Mother. When Pakal's elder son took over, the hieroglyphs would remind everyone that he was descended from the goddess of creation.

The grand old lady died in 640 CE. Pakal, now 44 years old, put the plan into action. Starting with additions to the royal palace, he began an impressive building program.

Pakal's structures were unlike any others in Mesoamerica. A delicate layer of red-painted stucco coated the thick stone walls. Multiple doors let sunlight in from all directions. Porches with high ceilings shaped like an upside-down V gave the buildings a feeling of lightness. Compared to other Mesoamerican structures, these were enchanted castles.

Pakal chose one space in the remodeled palace as a throne room. His men leaned a slab of stone more than four feet high and two feet wide against one wall. Then artists carved an oval picture of his mother giving him the crown years before.

In this drawing of a scene carved on the Oval Tablet of Palenque, Lady Sak K'uk' presents the headdress of rulership to her son, King Pakal. Glyphs above Lady Sak K'uk's head record her name, and glyphs on the right record Pakal's name.

When he was about 70, Pakal began the building that would clinch his mother's identity as First Mother: the Temple of Inscriptions. He located this beautiful pyramid-temple next to his palace, at the foot of a mountain. Mountains were sacred to the Maya, and Pakal's pyramid was an extension of the sacred mountain behind it. The stage was set for his mother's transformation to First Goddess. It was also set for Pakal's future burial.

Pakal knew he would need a tomb one day soon. His workers cleared the land and built a burial chamber on the bottom platform of the pyramid. Inside, they placed a sarcophagus, or stone coffin, for Pakal's body. The men built a steep staircase down into the pit so the tomb could easily be reached when he died. Then they erected the walls that would hold up the pyramid over the tomb. Against the back wall, they placed three limestone slabs.

The next step completed Lady Sak K'uk's extreme makeover. Pakal told scribes to engrave the slabs with 617 glyphs telling the history of his reign. One glyph recorded his mother's name, but this was no ordinary glyph. It was almost the same as the emblem glyph for Bone: a screaming bird, its beak filled with feathers.

The picture made perfect sense—when Lady Sak K'uk' gave Pakal the crown, she gave the city a way to regain its name. One last stroke of genius closed the deal. Those two glyphs were almost the same as the one for the First Mother, the goddess of creation. Visitors to the pyramid couldn't miss the message in front of their eyes: Pakal's mother and the goddess of creation were the same. Lady Sak K'uk' had thought of everything.

Pakal died in 683 at the ripe old age of 81. Following his wishes, his sons buried him in the sarcophagus. Carved portraits of his ancestors on all sides of the stone casket welcome him into the spirit world. Lady Sak K'uk's

A NEW LOOK AT OLD WRITING

Mexican archaeologist Alberto Ruz discovered Pakal's tomb in 1956. Since then, scholars have translated the hieroglyphs that Pakal and later rulers inscribed. They've found that Bone's written history is as long as those from ancient Egypt, Mesopotamia, and China.

Specialists at the National Museum of Anthropology in Mexico City carefully restored this jade mosaic mask, which was placed over Pakal's face when he was buried. Such masks were fashioned and buried so that the face of the king could live on for eternity.

Pakal's stone sarcophagus was set into a vaulted chamber and covered with a carved stone slab. This reconstruction in the National Museum of Anthropology in Mexico City allows visitors to see what his tomb looked like on the day he was laid to rest.

BONE AND ITS RULERS

599 CE
Calakmul attacks Bone

611 CE
Calakmul attacks Bone again

612 CE
Lady Sak K'uk' becomes queen

615 CE
Lady Sak K'uk' crowns 12-year-old Pakal

640 CE
Lady Sak K'uk' dies

647 CE
Pakal completes additions to his palace

673 CE
Pakal begins building the Temple of Inscriptions

683 CE
Pakal dies after reigning 67 years

picture appears twice—a double image that highlights the role she played in her son's rule.

Lady Sak K'uk' would have been pleased with what happened next. Pakal's elder son became king, and when he died, his younger brother took the throne. No one in Bone objected. Both sons built more temples, all containing slabs with glyphs that continued the history of Bone.

Pakal's building program made Bone a center of Maya art and architecture. And the glyphs in his Temple of Inscriptions make up one of longest written histories in ancient Mesoamerica. Both the buildings and the writing within allow him—and his mother—to live on in spirit forever.

CHAPTER 7

FEAR AND FIRE
THE FALL OF MAYA KINGDOMS

A SCRIBAL HOUSE, A SEASHELL ORNAMENT, AND HOLLOWED STONES

Sometime in the early 800s CE, hidden perhaps by dark of night, warriors invaded the Maya city of **Aguateca**. It was easier said than done. Since 1993, archaeologists have been studying the ruins of Aguateca. They know that high cliffs and a chasm 25 yards wide protected the city on one side. A series of walls protected it on the other. But the attackers were intent on destruction, and somehow they clambered over the walls. Their first target was a group of palace buildings in the heart of Aguateca.

agua + teca = "water" + "place" in the Spanish language

Archaeologists think it's likely that the royal family had already escaped. They also think that the family was hopeful they could return one day, because they left pots, tools, mirrors, and costly jade beads behind. The family stored these objects in a room and sealed the doorway with a stone wall.

The warriors must have been furious to find the palace deserted. They tore down the wall, threw the pots outside, and deliberately smashed them. As a final insult, they damaged the stone bench where the king would have sat. Then they set the entire group of palace build-

Mesoamerican people used clay figurines to play out dramas in homes and temples. The site in Aguateca, Guatemala, is rich with figurines. This example portrays a well-dressed nobleman, whose sparse but long beard and wrinkled brow indicate that he was an old man.

ings on fire. Aguateca was the capital city of a Maya king-dom and the seat of a family dynasty. By destroying its palace, the invaders hoped to destroy the power of the city itself—a mission so important that they didn't even bother to steal the jade beads.

Bol is a Maya man's name. The scribe carved his name on the ornament, but archaeologists are still working on the trans-lation of the glyph. Mean-while, we are calling him Bol.

What were the residents of Aguateca doing in the mean-time? It's hard to say. In 1993, archaeologist Takeshi Inomata excavated the home of **Bol** the Scribe. Bol's spacious five-room house was 120 yards from the palace—about the length of one football field. If the invasion began at night, perhaps he was asleep, worn out after a hard day's work. After all, Bol worked for the king. As the king's employee, the scribe was a man of privi-lege, but a busy one. And arti-facts that Inomata found in his workroom prove it.

[66] Scribal house, Aguateca, Guatemala, 800 CE

Bol carved shell ornaments and shaped ceramic flutes by hand. He even engraved a human skull with glyphs that described the king's crowning. When Bol wasn't carv-ing or engraving, he used red paint to decorate numerous pots with glyphs. Naturally, such a gifted artist would craft a few things for himself.

[66] Seashell ornament, Aguateca, Guatemala, 800 CE

Inomata found a seashell ornament carved with Bol's name and title. Apparently, the scribe was a modest fellow, because he engraved his self-portrait on the inside where no one could see it. For some reason, he was not wearing the ornament when the raid began. Maybe he removed it before falling asleep.

If Bol was sleeping, we can only imagine what woke him up. Victorious shouts? The bitter smell of smoke? The crackle of flaming thatch when warriors torched his roof? Whatever alarmed Bol, surely the ornament was the last thing on his mind, because he fled without it. He left his tools, too: hollowed-out stones for mixing paint, shell plates, and shell inkpots. He even left his precious greenstone beads behind.

We don't know what happened to Bol. Maybe he was taken prisoner, or perhaps the defensive walls beside his house saved him. One of the walls ran through Bol's patio, and another jutted into the front yard. Let's hope he leaped over the walls and fled to the outer ring of the city.

Here were the modest, one-room houses of plain folk with little wealth. The attackers had no interest in burning these huts, so the people could leave at their own pace. Takeshi Inomata thinks these commoners found other places to live—that they abandoned their homes gradually, moving a few belongings at a time.

Inomata also thinks some of the people must have left by canoe. Others would have traveled by foot, hauling their household goods on their backs. Foot travel probably meant several trips back to the smoldering city. By then, the attacking warriors had probably vanished, their mission accomplished. The one-room houses remained, and a few walls still stood. Otherwise, the city of Aguateca was a smoky memory.

Aguateca wasn't the only abandoned Maya city. From 800 to 900 CE, most cities in the southern lowlands were deserted one by one. Why did the Maya leave beautiful places like Copán and Palenque? These questions have fascinated researchers since the 19th century, when they first stumbled across ruins shrouded by centuries of jungle vines.

Some archaeologists thought a great drought or terrible disease must have plagued the people. Or if the Maya cut down too many trees for farming, erosion would have washed away the soil. With nothing to eat, the famished

Hollowed stones, Aguateca, Guatemala, 800 CE

people would have listened to their bellies and searched for fertile land. Other archaeologists suspected that warriors from central Mexico destroyed Maya cities.

In a way, all of the experts were wrong, and all of them were right. Scholars now realize that no one thing caused the ancient Maya kingdoms to collapse—a little of everything did. And what happened in one place may have been very different from what happened in another.

Anthropologist Rebecca Storey has studied skeletons from the city of Copán. Though she has a grisly job, she never lets it rattle her, and she has uncovered fascinating evidence. When Storey examined the skulls of Copán's ordinary people and royalty, she discovered signs of a condition called anemia. At best, this lack of red blood cells causes fatigue. At worst, it leads to death. Not enough iron in the diet can cause anemia, but royal families would have eaten well. So poor nutrition wasn't the reason they lacked red blood cells. Storey decided that an infectious disease led to widespread anemia in Copán. "It is an indication of how generally unhealthy the environment was for most Copanecos," she says.

Some archaeologists argue that outsiders from the western edge of the Maya world interrupted trade along the borders. Greedy for wealth, these outside traders could have kept necessities like salt and luxuries like cacao for making chocolate from reaching Maya kingdoms in the middle of the jungle. The disgruntled Maya might have wondered why they should bother living in a city.

War can destroy a civilization, too. Sometime after 550 CE, vandals set fire to the great temples of Teotihuacan, a city in central Mexico. Some archaeologists believe that vandals attacked Aguateca almost three centuries later for the same reason: to end the city's power as a sacred place.

During wartime, two Maya cities often joined forces against a more powerful city. It was a way of saying, "I'll help you fight, if you'll help me fight." Glyphs carved on stone monuments called stelae often tell about these alliances. The stelae explain arguments, list friendships with other cities, discuss triumphs and defeats, and describe taking prisoners of war. An alliance could mean victory for both, but sometimes it meant double defeat. This is what happened in Aguateca. It allied with another city, but when that one fell, Aguateca toppled next.

Imagine constant sickness in your house, or always fearing for your life. Imagine food without salt, or never tasting chocolate again. No wonder the Maya abandoned their great cities, though they didn't all leave at once. Some people clung desperately to the belief that their king was related to the gods—that when he made offerings, the deities would grant bountiful harvests and good health.

But finally, it seems, the Maya couldn't stand the uncertainty of life in southern lowland cities. They voted with their feet and moved to unspoiled forests. Here they could live a simpler, more peaceful life—the life their ancestors lived before kings came along, claiming to be related to the gods. Their flight seems like a sad ending to the magnificent Maya art and architecture that flourished for over 1,100 years. Still, the end of one thing is often the beginning of another.

The Maya have continued their culture over the centuries. More than six million people still speak one of 39 Mayan languages. Many Maya combine Christian worship with the old tradition of offering food and drink to the ancient gods. Some still make pottery painted with red designs, just as Bol the Scribe did 1,000 years ago.

Maya culture didn't die with its cities. Like ancient cultures in China, the Middle East, and Europe that live on in a modern form, the Maya way of life survives in language, religious customs, and art.

LATER, IN NORTH AMERICA

Five centuries after Aguateca burned, a group of Native Americans called the Mogollon were living in an 18-room adobe house in central Arizona. In 1300 CE, they or someone else set fire to the house. The residents threw dirt and trash on the blaze, and then fled. They left most of their belongings on the floor, including 300 pots.

Archaeologists are still trying to understand the reason for the rapid abandonment of this house. The area had been suffering from a great drought for 25 years, so perhaps the Mogollon decided to search for a place with rainfall. By setting a ritual fire, they could erase bad memories and start a new life somewhere else.

CHAPTER 8

" FERDINAND
COLUMBUS AND
THE BOOK OF
CHILAM BALAM OF
CHUMAYEL

COTTON, COPPER, AND CANOES
THE RISE OF THE PUTÚN MAYA AT CHICHÉN ITZÁ

In the summer of 1502, Admiral Christopher Columbus was 51 years old and lost again. Now leading his fourth expedition to the Americas, the Italian explorer was still searching for a trade route to Asia. With him were 140 sailors, his brother, Bartholomew, and his 13-year-old son, Ferdinand.

One day in July, Columbus anchored his four ships 36 miles from modern-day Honduras. The admiral sent his brother out in a small boat to explore a nearby island. When Bartholomew spotted a huge Maya trading canoe, he hailed it over to the main ship. Ferdinand must have been watching from the deck, because after he grew up he described the scene in a book he wrote about his father.

" Ferdinand Columbus, *The Life of the Admiral*, 16th century CE

[It was as] long as a galley [100 feet] and eight feet wide, made of a single tree trunk . . . it had a palm-leaf awning . . . this gave complete protection against the rain and waves. Under this awning were the children and women and all the baggage and merchandise. There were twenty-five paddlers. . . . [The Admiral] took aboard the costliest and handsomest things in that cargo: cotton mantles and sleeveless shirts embroidered and painted in different designs and colors . . . knives that cut like steel; hatchets . . . made of good copper. . . . For provisions they had . . . wine made of maize.

Archaeologists digging in Mesoamerica have uncovered the same kinds of goods that Ferdinand saw that day. They know now that the Maya had traded such merchandise for hundreds of years. But to Ferdinand, the contents of the vessel must have seemed wonderfully new and strange.

Scholars also know from paintings in native history books that the Maya had been making canoes for centuries before Ferdinand saw them. But he had no way of knowing that enormous dugout canoes were old hat to the Maya. And the boy certainly didn't know the fascinating history of the Maya seafaring trade.

Much of that history concerns the city of Chichén Itzá. Chichén Itzá is 50 miles inland from the tip of the thumb-shaped Yucatán peninsula. Before 900 CE, it was a typical Maya farming city. But that changed in 918 CE, when a different group of Maya called the Putún sailed to Isla Cerritos, a trading city on an island at the top of the thumb. Then they hiked overland to Chichén Itzá.

The Putún were Mayan speakers, but their shoulder capes, cropped bangs, and long hair seemed foreign to people in Chichén Itzá. These strangers worshipped the

One of many dramatic, finely wrought buildings in Chichén Itzá is the Temple of the Warriors. The Temple is covered in intricate relief carvings. This one shows Maya warriors and eagles and jaguars devouring human hearts.

Feathered Serpent, a god seldom honored in the city. Even their speech sounded peculiar. Five centuries later, an unnamed Maya scribe wrote *The Book of Chilam Balam of Chumayel*. In it, he described the Putún as those who "speak our language brokenly."

What did the Putún want? The answer is seafaring trade, and the Putún were already masters of it. Expert watermen, they came from a swampy region called Tabasco. Unlike Columbus, who never found his shortcut to Asia, the Putún Maya knew Yucatán water routes backwards and forwards.

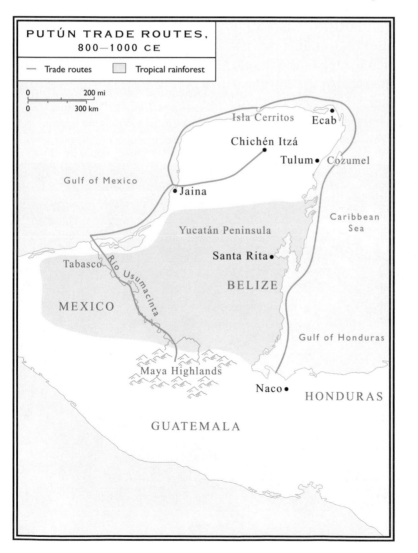

Tabasco is midway between highlands to the west, tropical rainforests in the south, and the Yucatán Peninsula. The central position made it easy to trade goods with highland cities, then swap them elsewhere in Mesoamerica.

Eager to expand their business, the Putún made deals with highland merchants. They convinced them it was foolish to haul goods slowly overland on the backs of porters. Moving goods more quickly by water was much more efficient. After all, quick sales would mean quick profits. It was an offer that highland traders couldn't refuse.

Another trade opportunity landed in the Putún's lap between 800 and 900 CE. Throughout that century, warring Maya kings in the southern tropical rainforests

burned and sacked each other's cities. When endless warfare interrupted trade, the Putún stepped in and took over
a necklace of cities around the Yucatán Peninsula. Control
of the seaports meant they could move goods around the
coast within days. Now all they needed was a central site
that connected the cities. Chichén Itzá was just the spot.

And what did the people in Chichén Itzá think of
this plan? They weren't sold on the idea. Murals in the city's
temples show that the Putún Maya
and Yucatán Maya fought *mano
a mano*, or hand-to-hand, in several battles.

An art historian has studied
the murals and assigned nick-
names to each leader. Captain
Serpent and his Putún troops
carry round shields painted with
dots. Captain Sun Disk, the leader
of Chichén Itzá, heads a company of
men who carry rectangular shields.

One mural shows a battle that takes
place in a village south of the city.
Warriors are painted in various fighting poses. Some swing from vines, while
others launch darts from the
tops of towers. The mural
painter included the forgotten
victims of war, too. Women
wearing knapsacks are fleeing
the scene. One seems to be
crying; another lifts her hand
in anguish toward the home
she might never see again.
Who won the war? The proof is
in the murals: in one of the
temples, two painted scenes
over a doorway show Captain
Serpent removing the hearts of
defeated warriors.

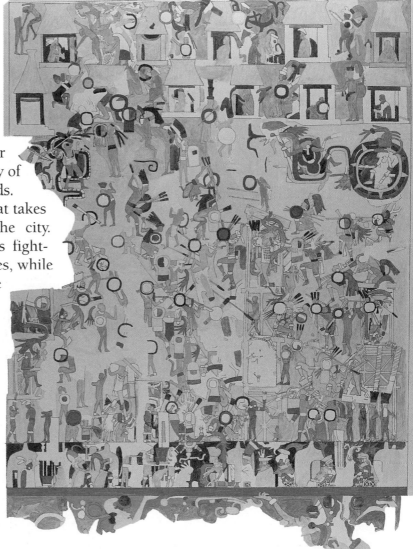

*This mural at the Great Ballcourt of
Chichén Itzá is the only known record
of an epic battle between Captain Sun
Disk (at top right, with the large circular Sun Disk behind him) and Captain
Serpent (at top left, with a large serpent body winding around him).*

The triumphant Putún could now get down to business. Archaeologists know that people in Chichén Itzá raised corn and cotton and harvested cacao pods. While excavating ancient warehouses in the city, archaeologists have also found goods from other places in Mesoamerica: copper, seashells, and orange pottery. The digs show that the shrewd Putún turned Chichén Itzá into a shopping district as lively as any mall.

Follow the typical journey of a shipment of ceramic bowls, and you can see how the Putún spun their web of trade. One day in Tabasco, a Putún trader might exchange cacao pods for a large shipment of bowls made by women in the highlands. The bowls are pale orange, lovely as a sunset. The hypothetical trader is certain he can sell them. The next morning, he mans his canoe with slaves and outfits it with a cotton-cloth sail.

The canoe would head up the west coast of the Yucatán Peninsula. With the help of hired porters, the slaves haul the goods inland down to Chichén Itzá.

Perhaps on the following day, the trader displays his bowls at the city's market. It could be that a woman who weaves cloaks has displayed her handiwork, too: fine cloaks with feather work and embroidery, and plain white cotton cloths that are as valuable as money in ancient Mesoamerica. She happily trades her piles of cloaks for the beautiful orange bowls.

The next day, the Putún trader rounds up the slaves and porters. They carry the cloaks on their backs up to the coast and load them into his canoe. Then he and the crew might head to Isla Cerritos, which has some of the richest salt beds in Mesoamerica. There, the merchant trades his cloaks for blocks of salt.

Leaving Isla Cerritos behind, the trader would navigate around the tip of the peninsula and turn south. Then the canoe would dock at the island of Cozumel, another important center of trade. The trader might barter his salt for spiny oyster shells from the Pacific Ocean. People all over Mesoamerica use the shells for making jewelry, so heavy demand makes them as valuable as cloaks, cacao, and jade.

SLAVERY IN MESOAMERICA

A Mesoamerican man who was in debt could sell himself into slavery for a certain amount of time, even for life. Some became house servants. Others labored in the fields raising crops or managed large farms. Unlike the system of slavery that developed after the Europeans arrived, Mesoamerican slaves could own property and even other slaves.

If a husband needed money, he might sell his wife, or poor parents might sell their children. Kings could turn a young girl into a slave and present her as a gift to another ruler. Prisoners of war became slaves, but not for long. Warriors took them back to the temple in their city, where priests sacrificed them as offerings to the gods.

Now it's time to head back home to Tabasco. There, the merchant could easily exchange the oyster shells for more orange ware, and the circle of trade would begin again.

The Putún brought more than trade to the northern lowland city of Chichén Itzá. Over time, people accepted their strange ways. Archaeologists aren't sure why. Some think military might is the only reason. Others think smooth talking and new wealth in the city helped, too.

People in Chichén Itzá did manage to keep their belief in a rain god. Every year, thousands of pilgrims traveled there so they could throw offerings into a natural rock well called a *cenote*. Archaeologists have pulled pottery, incense, jade, gold, and animal remains from the well. They've even found human bones. When worshippers tossed a person into the water, they hoped he would live so that he could bring back a prophecy from the rain god. It seems like an unusual way of predicting the weather. But people were anxious to know what the future held, because rainfall meant a good harvest and enough food to survive the next year.

Though belief in the rain god persisted, ruins in Chichén Itzá prove that the Putún got their way on most other things. Archaeologists know that the seamen were fond of architectural columns used by their trading buddies in the highlands, because similar columns hold up temples in Chichén Itzá. Outside one pyramid, a forest of stone columns seems to sprout from the ground. Each column bears the portrait of a warrior and his name glyph. The Putún covered these columns with a thatched roof, creating an open-air room called a colonnade.

HOW TO HUG A SHORE

The Putún kept their canoes close to the coastline, where the ocean was calm. That way they could avoid crashing into rocky reefs farther offshore. Traveling one day at a time, they made short runs from place to place. Flat beaches along the Yucatán Peninsula had no natural landmarks, so the sailors depended on guidance from land.

People along the shore lit bonfires or climbed trees with a torch and sent clouds of smoke into the air. Other helpers ran along the shoreline waving flags, or they put up feather banners to mark a landing spot. These signals alerted sailors to a quiet bay where they could beach the canoe and rest their aching arms for the night.

This disk and other gold objects were thrown into the cenote, or great well, at Chichén Itzá as offerings to the rain god, Chac. The two warriors embossed on the disk are fighting a battle.

Buildings in Chichén Itzá show that eventually people accepted the idea of the Feathered Serpent god. His carved face peers sternly from columns, stairways, and doorways of temples built after the Putún arrived. The residents of Chichén Itzá even built a magnificent pyramid that allowed the Feathered Serpent god to reveal himself twice a year. The pyramid has nine stepped levels. At sunrise on the first days of spring and fall, the nine levels cast a shadow that curves, snake-like, down the edge of the pyramid staircase.

The Feathered Serpent god proved to be a good traveler over distance and time. The idea of worshipping a rattlesnake covered with feathers began with the Olmec in

Giant feathered serpents with rattles and gaping jaws guard the central doorway at the Temple of the Warriors in Chichén Itzá. Such sculptures are evidence that the Feathered Serpent cult became very popular throughout Mesoamerica in the 9th century CE.

The Temple of the Warriors, the largest structure at Chichén Itzá, was decorated with stone sculptures that portrayed gods and heroes. Columns at the base of the pyramid are carved with portraits of warriors, who are identified by their hieroglyphic names.

500 BCE. Five centuries later, the belief moved north, where people in Teotihuacan built a huge pyramid covered with carvings of feathered snakes. Then he slithered south to the city of Copán, deep in Maya territory.

Sometimes the Feathered Serpent was the god of war; sometimes he was the god of merchants. A sculpture might show him coiled like a corkscrew or with a human face between his jaws. The Maya called him Kukulcan, while people who spoke Nahuatl called him **Quetzalcoatl**. But whatever form or name people gave him, the Feathered Serpent was a sign of power and command throughout ancient Mesoamerica.

{ *quetzal* + *coatl* (ket-zahl-KO-aht) = "feathered" + "serpent" in Nahuatl

CHAPTER 9

" FRAY BERNARDINO DE SAHAGÚN, NAHUATL POEM, AND COLUMNS IN TULA GRANDE

THE FEATHERED SERPENT RIDES AGAIN
THE CITY OF TULA

Historians have nicknamed him TQ, for Topiltzin Quetzalcoatl. Who was this TQ? A wizard or a king? A god named Quetzalcoatl, or a priest serving that god? Did TQ found the city of Tula, or did he rule its people, the Toltec? It's hard to tell. We do know that ancient Mesoamericans always pictured TQ as a feathered serpent. And we know he was a symbol of supreme rule throughout Mesoamerica.

TQ was so important that people told at least six different legends about him.

In the 16th century CE, a native Mesoamerican dictated one of these legends to a Spanish priest named Bernardino de Sahagún. The speaker used his native language and included a wealth of detail, so historians think his account is the most useful of the written versions. In Sahagún's book, the legend is titled "Third Chapter, which tells the tale of Quetzalcoatl, who was a great wizard and of the place where he ruled, and of what he did when he went away."

Topiltzin Quetzalcoatl (Our Prince, Feathered Serpent) draws his own blood to offer to the gods as his most precious gift. Nearly 600 years after the legendary ruler died, an Aztec scribe painted this portrait of him.

The legend explains that "This Quetzalcoatl they considered as a god; he was thought a god; he was prayed to in olden times there at Tula." The native speaker who dictated the story didn't say when TQ arrived. But archaeological digs show that Tula was built in central Mexico between 700 and 900 CE. If TQ was a real man, he lived in the city sometime during those years.

During these ancient times, Tula's streets and neighborhoods covered two square miles. A towering temple with numerous steps stood in a main plaza in the center of the city. Details of the legend are vague, but somewhere on the temple a sculptor carved TQ's image: a bearded face so ugly that the artist hid it from view.

TQ's face might have been repulsive to the Toltecs, but they built handsome palaces for him. Though archaeologists haven't found these buildings yet, the legend says, "And there stood his green stone house, and his golden house, and his seashell house, and his snail shell house, and his house of beams, his turquoise house, and his house of precious feathers." The feathers on the walls of this last palace were yellow, blue, green, and white: the rainbow plumage of the sacred quetzal bird.

The story states that TQ ruled wisely from these splendid homes. He bathed in the chilly midnight air as penance when he thought he had offended the gods. And he commanded that his priests sacrifice only serpents and butterflies, not human beings. "And the . . . priests took their manner of conduct from the life of Quetzalcoatl," the legend states. "By it they established the law of Tula. Thus were customs established here in Mexico."

In return for TQ's wisdom, the Toltecs turned Tula into an artistic center where craftspeople created sculptures of feathered serpents, beautiful feathered

66 Fray Bernardino de Sahagún, *Florentine Codex*, 16th century CE

BERNARDINO'S BIG BOOK

In the 16th century CE, a Spanish priest named Fray Bernardino de Sahagún was worried that people would forget what Mesoamerica had been like before the Spaniards arrived in 1519 CE. With the help of native translators and scribes, the priest made a written record of 40 speeches that native Mesoamericans gave on special occasions. He also asked 13 native speakers to explain their history, religion, and customs. They illustrated their descriptions with simple but moving drawings.

Eventually the priest put all his information in one codex, or bound book. This original codex was lost, but someone found a copy years later. Over the next five centuries, scholars made more copies from this one. The best has 1,210 leaves (a leaf is the front and back of one page) and 1,846 color illustrations. Around 1588, this superior copy made its way to a museum in Florence, Italy, though no one knows how it got there. Other Spanish priests and Mesoamerican scribes wrote histories, but the *Florentine Codex* is the longest. It is our time machine back to the great civilizations before the Spanish conquest.

A Toltec warrior emerges from the jaws of a coyote. Four inches tall and inlaid with miniature pieces of mother-of-pearl shell, the clay sculpture is an outstanding example of craftsmanship in the city of Tula.

headdresses, and monumental public buildings. Tula was so famous for its art that Mesoamericans honored the city by calling it Tollan, or Place of the Reeds. In Nahuatl, this means it was a civilized place.

The legend in Sahagún's book says the Toltecs gave TQ credit for their masterful craftsmanship: "Nothing was difficult when they [the Toltec] did it, when they cut the green stone and cast gold, and made still other works of the craftsman, of the feather worker. Very highly skilled were they. Indeed these crafts started . . . from Quetzalcoatl."

When storytellers pass a tale down through the centuries, facts can turn into fantasy. Over time, Tula became a heavenly place, where ears of maize grew so big that people could barely hold them in their arms. Cotton sprouted from the ground in rich colors of chili red, deep yellow, and coyote brown. "All of these came forth exactly so," the story goes, " . . . they did not dye them."

In blissful Tula, a choir of singing birds flew through the air, cheering up all who heard their sweet songs. An abundance of cacao plants made the tasty cocoa drink available to everyone. Gold and green stones were so inexpensive that all the people were rich, and no one needed anything.

Tula sounds like paradise. In reality, it was a fashionable and comfortable place to live. Unfortunately, it lasted only 200 years. After studying the city's ruins, archaeologists are certain that the original city burned shortly before 900 CE. Who would destroy this glorious place, and why?

Sahagún's book offers some clues. It states that three of TQ's priests changed their loyalty from TQ to Smoking

---

**A TALE OF
TWO TULAS**

700–900 CE
Toltecs build Tula
Chico

900 CE
Tula Chico burns

950 CE
Toltecs build Tula
Grande

1150 CE
Tula Grande is a major
Mesoamerican city

1200 CE
Tula Grande residents
move to Valley of
Mexico

Mirror, a god of war. Here reality turns again into a tall tale. The priests are wizards who torment TQ by tricking him into drinking a magic potion that makes him drunk. And they hold a disastrous puppet show: when curious Toltecs dash forward to see the puppets, they crush each other to death.

Defeated by the wily priests, **Topiltzin Quetzalcoatl** burns his temple and flees the city. But first the priest-god enjoys some revenge. Before leaving, he changes the cacao plants into scratchy mesquite bushes. Then he orders the singing birds to abandon Tula and fly to the Gulf of Mexico. Mourning the loss of his city, TQ leaves. A Nahuatl poem tells us about the exile's grief:

{ topiltzin + quetzalcoatl (toe-PEEL-tzeen ket-zahl-CO-aht) = "Our Prince" + "Feathered Serpent" in Nahuatl

> Then he [Quetzalcoatl] fixes his eyes on Tula and in
>   that moment begins to weep:
> as he weeps sobbing, it is like two torrents of hail
>   trickling down:
> His tears slip down his face;
> His tears drop by drop perforate [pierce] the stones.

66 Nahuatl poem

The legend says that most of Tula's people remained loyal to their leader. After he was cast out, they buried their wealth. Then they gathered their families—the children, the ailing, and the elderly—and followed TQ to the coast. Here, the legend says, "he made a raft of serpents. . . . Thereupon he went off; he went swept off by the water." As the raft soared east over the Atlantic Ocean, TQ vowed to return from the east in the year One Reed. According to the sacred Mesoamerican calendar, this was the anniversary year of TQ's birthday.

66 Fray Bernardino de Sahagún, *Florentine Codex*, 16th century CE

Meanwhile in Tula, the people rebuilt a new plaza some distance from TQ's burned temple. Archaeologists have discovered that as the new city spread, it surrounded the old ruins. But no one ever built over them. TQ's remaining supporters may have preserved the space, hoping that he would reappear.

Archaeologists now call the old city Tula Chico, or Small Tula, and the rebuilt city Tula Grande, or Big Tula. By 950 CE, Tula Grande covered about five square miles. By

"They say he [TQ] traveled to the east . . . and that he was summoned by the sun. And they say he is still alive and that he is to reign again and rebuild that city which [his enemies] destroyed. And so to this day they await him."

Fray Bernardino de Sahagún, *Florentine Codex*, 16th century CE

1150 CE, between 60,000 and 80,000 people hung their headdresses there. Archaeologists have found obsidian tools, pottery, and jewelry in the city, suggesting that Tula Grande remained a center of the arts.

Still, the peaceful old days were gone. Archaeologists also found gruesome skull racks that display the heads of prisoners of war. Processions of carved warriors march across the fronts of stone benches. Columns are carved with warrior-like men and their name glyphs. Tula didn't completely forget TQ, because a feathered serpent image decorates one of these columns. But it's clear that after he fled, the people switched their loyalty to gods of war and human sacrifice.

‟ Columns in Tula Grande, 950 CE

Tula Grande reminds archaeologists of Teotihuacan, the renowned Mesoamerican city that enemies partly burned around 600 CE. The two pyramids in Tula Grande were built at a 90-degree angle to one another, just like the Sun and Moon pyramids of Teotihuacan. The patios and porches of Tula's houses look like ones in Teotihuacan's apartment compounds. The art is similar, too. One carved warrior in Tula wears the goggles of the Storm God. Artists in Teotihuacan frequently painted this god on murals.

Most archaeologists think the Toltecs who rebuilt Tula deliberately imitated the art and architecture of Teotihuacan. The two cities are only 50 miles apart and connected by a natural corridor. People in Tula Grande might easily have visited Teotihuacan and wanted to copy its massive pyramids. Just as ancient Romans copied the classic art and architecture of Greece, Tula claimed a legacy from the sacred and powerful Teotihuacan.

Sadly, the two cities shared more than art and architecture. Teotihuacan ended in 900 CE, and Tula collapsed around 1150 CE.

Mexican archaeologists in Tula Grande dug and restored Pyramid B, one of the finest examples of Toltec architecture and sculpture. Heroic Toltec warriors are carved into the great stone columns, which supported an elaborately carved and painted flat roof, the largest of its day in Mesoamerica.

Scientists think that the climate in Mexico around that time was cooler and wetter than usual, so perhaps flooding caused crop failure. Whatever happened, Tula's ruler tried to start a new city to the south. The plan failed when he died. His people split into bands who wandered farther south into the Valley of Mexico.

The refugees never forgot the magnificent Tula. For the next 500 years, their descendants proudly claimed that they were related to the Toltec. They considered themselves royalty, and only men from their royal line could rule in the Valley of Mexico. Then a little-known people from northern Mesoamerica arrived. The powerful Aztec Empire was about to begin.

MEANWHILE, IN NORTH AMERICA

Around 1150 CE, Toltec influence spread to North America. Native Americans in the states we now call Alabama, Georgia, Tennessee, and Illinois built huge temple mounds and plazas similar to those in Tula.

CHAPTER 10

TRIPLE WHAMMY
FORGING THE AZTEC EMPIRE

aztlán = "island in the middle of a lake" in Nahuatl. Aztlán led to Aztec, a catch-all term referring to many groups of people who lived in the empire, including the Mexica.

‶ Aztec myth recorded by Fray Diego Durán, *The History of the Indies of New Spain,* 1581 CE

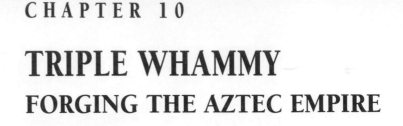

This stone sculpture of an eagle perched on a cactus is carved with the date 1325. The Aztec high god Huitzilopochtli told his people to build a temple on the spot where they saw an eagle perched on a cactus in the middle of a lake. Legend has it that they sighted this omen in 1325 CE and built the temple to their high god on that spot, surrounding it with their capital city of Tenochtitlan.

In the 16th century, a Spanish priest named Diego Durán interviewed descendants of people who called themselves the Mexica. Their ancestors had passed down a myth about coming to the Valley of Mexico, and Durán recorded the tale.

The myth states that sometime around 1000 CE, a humble people from **Aztlán**, a mythical place in northeastern Mexico, were contacted by the god Mexi. Mexi told them to leave their homeland. They should stop wandering when they saw a special cactus. "This cactus is so tall and splendid that an eagle makes his nest in it," the myth says. "Each day the eagle in his nest feeds here, eating the finest and most beautiful birds he can find . . . all around it you will see the innumerable green, blue, red, yellow, and white feathers from the splendid birds on which the eagle feeds."

The people obeyed. For 200 years, groups of people left Aztlán, then changed their name to Mexica in honor of Mexi. The last cluster of weary travelers reached a series of connected lakes in what is now central Mexico. There, on an island in the largest lake, they saw the sign that Mexi had prophesied: a cactus plant with a bird on top.

Thankful that their journey was over, the Mexica made their home on the western side of Lake Texcoco. It wasn't easy, because the cactus grew in a rocky, watery marsh. The people struggled, hauling earth and rocks from the shores of the lake to fill in the marsh. But they persisted, and when their numbers multiplied, they organized themselves into neighborhood clans with elected leaders.

According to the myth recorded by Durán, a Mexica priest gave instructions about naming the city. "Our god orders us to call this place Tenochtitlan," the priest told the people. "There will be built the city that is to

Diego Rivera is considered the finest Mexican painter of the 20th century, best known for his dramatic murals of daily life in both modern and ancient Mexico. The foreground of his painting of ancient Tenochtitlan depicts the great market. The orderly canals, causeways, and temples that astounded the Spaniards are in the background.

be queen, that is to rule over all others in the country. There we shall receive other kings and nobles, who will recognize Tenochtitlan as the supreme capital."

The Mexica prospered. By 1367 CE, they had built a small island kingdom and were vassals, or servants, of the nearby Tepanec kingdom. But two neighboring cities, Tlacopan and Texcoco, regarded Tenochtitlan as an upstart. Royal families in both places claimed to be descended from the Toltec of Tula. They despised the Mexica as barbarians.

The Mexica were determined to find acceptance in their new homeland. When the rulers of Tepanec rewarded them with fertile fields in exchange for loyal service, their status increased. They even managed to marry one of their daughters to a Toltec prince in a nearby town. Slowly but surely, old-timers in the valley accepted the ambitious newcomers.

Then a bully took over the Tepanec throne. He killed or exiled members of royal families in Texcoco and Tlacopan and replaced them with lackeys who would do his bidding. The Tepanec king was harsh to the Mexica, too, and that was a fatal error. The strong-willed Mexica had not

MEMORIES AND MANUSCRIPTS

The Spanish conquered Tenochtitlan in 1521 CE. Twenty-one years later, a seven-year-old Spanish boy named Diego Durán moved to Mexico with his parents. A curious child, Durán was fascinated by the people of Tenochtitlan and their beliefs. After he grew up, he became a priest and interviewed elderly native people about their traditions. He recorded their memories in a three-part book about vanishing Aztec customs. These handwritten manuscripts are stored in a library in Spain. Now they serve as a spyglass that lets us glimpse the Aztec past.

struggled through the difficult years of building their kingdom to give up everything now.

In 1428 CE, Tenochtitlan, Texcoco, and Tlacopan made a pact that historians call the Triple Alliance. In a triple-whammy attack, warriors from the three *T* cities drove the Tepanec tyrants from their kingdom. With this victory, **Itzcoatl**, the Mexica king, suddenly found himself triumphant over his old masters. He was now also joint ruler of the entire Valley of Mexico.

The first thing Itzcoatl did was encourage the royal families of Texcoco and Tlacopan to return to their cities. Determined that royalty would never snub the Mexica again, he made sure that Mexica sons and daughters married into these royal families. This meant that the newly married Mexica and their children were royalty, too.

Rulers of the Triple Alliance cities divided the wealth of the Tepanec kingdom. Then they made a business agreement. They would wage wars on other kings in the region, forcing them to hand over jade, feathers, crafts, and crops. The *T* cities would divide the spoils of war, but whoever led the battle would receive the biggest share. The Mexica were eager fighters. They roared into combat first and fought the hardest, so most of the spoils went to Itzcoatl. Within 50 years, Tenochtitlan was the most powerful of the three cities in the Triple Alliance. The Aztec Empire had begun.

To maintain their war machine, the Mexica needed large families who would produce fighting men. Big families require

itz + coatl = "obsidian"+ "serpent" in Nahuatl

Canoes and boats still travel between chinampas, *or floating gardens, of Lake Xochimilco in the Valley of Mexico. In Aztec times, as now, women took flowers and other produce to market, paddling past tall willow trees that anchored the beds of stone and soil to the lake bottom.*

lots of food, so the Mexica looked to a region of freshwater lakes south of Tenochtitlan, where for hundreds of years people had been cultivating raised fields, or *chinampas*. They soon conquered this area and improved the *chinampas*. The Mexica first planted willow trees in the shallow lakebed, lined the areas between the trees with rocks and filled in the enclosures with earth. Night soil, or human excrement, was used as fertilizer. When earth in the narrow rectangular fields sank, the Mexica simply dug more from the bottom of the lake and threw it on top. This rich soil produced crops of maize, beans, and squash, all in the same year.

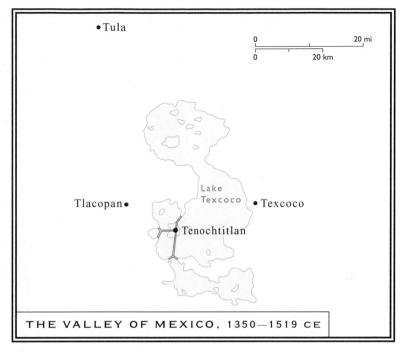

THE VALLEY OF MEXICO, 1350—1519 CE

Colorful flowers—spiky purple salvia and 20-foot-high dahlias—flourished in the raised fields, too. The Mexica grew so many flowers that they sent hundreds of canoes filled with blossoms to the marketplace every day.

Land, food, royal marriages, warrior-sons, the spoils of war, an endless supply of flowers for trade . . . what more could the Mexica want? But it wasn't enough. Itzcoatl worried that he and his nobles would have to share their riches with non-royal Mexica.

To solve the problem, he came up with a triple whammy of his own. First, he and a nephew who had the strange-sounding title of Serpent Woman rewrote the history of the Mexica. The new text explained why only the king and royal families should possess wealth.

Native people in Mexico retold this history for Diego Durán in the 16th century. In Itzcoatl's version of history, commoners had refused to fight the Tepanec, promising, "if you are victorious, we will serve you and work your lands

❝ Aztec myth

for you. We will pay tribute [taxes] to you, we will build your houses and be your servants . . . in short, we will sell and subject our persons and goods to your service forever."

It was all lies, of course, but writing them down made them seem true. With this propaganda, Itzcoatl and Serpent Woman remade the old neighborhood clans and created a top-to-bottom class structure. Think of it as a pyramid. The king perched on top, the nobles were just below, and commoners—most of the population—were underneath them all.

Itzcoatl made laws saying only nobles could wear shoes and cotton clothing or enjoy the delicious cold chocolate drink. Only nobles could live in two-story houses and marry multiple wives. Noble children attended schools where they read the "correct" history. Commoners could send their children to schools, too, but these children weren't taught the new history. So, if any of them grew up and became priests, the king labeled them evil carriers of false wisdom. Any commoner who dared to dress well or even wear jewelry was put to death. And though everyone had to pay tribute—flowers, crops, cloth—to the king, nobles paid less than commoners did.

Itzcoatl's second trick involved a god called Hummingbird on the Left. Some historians think he was similar to Mexi, or perhaps Mexi with a different name. Serpent Woman rewrote this god's story, too—he made him the center of a national religion that called for massive human sacrifice.

The idea behind the new myth was simple. As god of the sun, Hummingbird on the Left fought his way across the sky every day, waging battle with his brothers, the stars, and his sister, the moon. To stay strong for combat, he needed a magic substance found only in human blood. His daily requirement must be met, or the sun wouldn't rise. Thousands of commoners died believing that their deaths kept the sun in the sky.

In a painted illustration from a 16th-century codex, Huitzilopochtli (Hummingbird on the Left) carries a feathered shield in one hand and a fire serpent spear in the other. The fire serpent was the magic weapon that this sun and war god used to strike down his enemies in battle.

The king now had almost total control over the lower class. One last detail remained. Itzcoatl burned existing histories of the Mexica, leaving only the new version. Luckily, people in the older city of Texcoco hid their history books. Truth about the Mexicas' humble beginnings as drifting wanderers eventually came out.

Truth about book burning surfaced, too. In the 16th century, Durán recorded the Mexica story of what Itzcoatl and Serpent Woman had done. "They [Itzcoatl and Serpent Woman] said: 'It is not necessary for all the common people to know of the [writing] . . . for it containeth many falsehoods.'" By destroying the true history and writing a false one, Itzcoatl had erased an inconvenient past.

To strengthen his empire, Itzcoatl continued to arrange marriages with royal families in other cities. Those families pledged loyalty to him. But if a royal family refused to pay tribute, he killed them and put one of his own princes on the city's throne.

Itzcoatl did what rulers of great empires have done throughout history: expand the empire's territory as quickly as possible. He sent traders beyond the Valley of Mexico to acquire goods, and they acted as undercover agents, sniffing out prosperous kingdoms that owned fertile land and luxury goods. When the spies returned to Tenochtitlan with the information, Itzcoatl ordered armed warriors to visit the kingdoms. Their weapons delivered a message as clear as the water in Lake Texcoco: pay tribute to the king, or we'll use force.

Kings who ruled after Itzcoatl demanded even more tribute. After a while, angry commoners began to rebel against the system. Each time, the ruling king squashed the uprising. Like a mighty tree, the Aztec Empire spread its power through most of Mesoamerica. By the 16th century, it was exploiting kingdoms from the Gulf of Mexico to the Pacific Ocean, from northern highlands to tropical rainforests. Most scholars believe the empire would have kept growing. But in 1519, the Spanish conquerors arrived. The Aztec world would never be the same again.

STICKS AND STONES

There were two kinds of warriors in the Aztec empire: nobles trained in special schools and commoners who could rise to noble status by performing well in battle. For hand-to-hand combat, they used swords and wooden spears. If the enemy was yards away, they slung stones or launched darts using a stick called an *atlatl*. Warriors carried round wooden shields and wore quilted cotton armor to protect themselves.

Ancient Mesoamericans had no beasts of burden, so armies traveled by foot at about the rate of 1.4 miles per hour. They fought during the dry season, which runs from early December to late April in central Mexico. Aztec armies seldom worried about supplies when they marched toward an outlying kingdom—the emperor commanded every city along the way to provide his men with food.

CHAPTER 11

FLOWERS AND SONG
THE LIVES OF AZTEC FAMILIES

It's easy to remember the Aztec Empire for fabulous wealth, human sacrifices, and powerful rulers such as Itzcoatl. But those are only broad strokes on half of a painting. For a complete picture, you should spend time with ordinary Mexica. In the 16th century, the Spanish priest Bernardino de Sahagún asked native scribes to write down memories of life before the Spaniards arrived. Their words will help you go back in time to 1484 CE.

You're watching a hypothetical family in Tenochtitlan, the largest of three capital cities in the empire. Two parents and four children are living in an adobe house on a man-made island near the great marketplace. Nantli, or "Mother" in Nahuatl, inherited the land and kept her mother's last name. Nantli is the master of this home. On a typical day, she cooks tortillas, weeds the vegetable garden next to the house, and weaves and embroiders cloth for trade at the market.

The upper batten, or rod, on this loom holds weft (horizontal) threads in place as the woman pulls a warp (vertical) thread through with the lower batten. Most women in the Aztec empire contributed to household income by spinning and weaving.

A life-sized terracotta statue of an Aztec Eagle Warrior, the highest military rank within the Aztec imperial army, was found in the House of Eagles in Tenochtitlan. Shattered when the Spaniards invaded in 1521, the statue was reconstructed with painstaking care by experts in Mexico.

Tahtli, or Father, is a warrior in the emperor's army. He wears breeches and a cape with a design that indicates his rank of sergeant—a position based on the number of captives he has taken in battle and brought back for sacrifice at a temple.

Tahtli can capture only someone of his rank or higher—to capture anyone lower would be a humiliation. Most likely, he's proud that with each battle he's overcome men in higher positions, working his way up from private to corporal to sergeant. But fighting is only one of Tahtli's jobs. He probably has another trade, such as stone working or blacksmithing, or he works in *chinampas* outside the city.

Nantli and Tahtli have three sons, ages five, six, and eight. On a normal day, they might be at the marketplace with their mother, eyeing playthings at the toy stand. But this is not an ordinary day. Nantli has recently given birth to a fine baby girl. According to Sahagún's scribes, the midwife would have given a war cry when the baby "had arrived on earth." The yell announced that the Nantli fought a brave battle while giving birth. Now, one month later, she is dressing her infant in a little skirt for an important ceremony.

In the 16th century, one of Sahagún's scribes recalled the custom that Mexica families followed: "And while the baby yet lay [in the cradle], those who desired, those who loved [their] children, in order, it was said, that the baby would not quickly die, declared it to be for the temple. . . . Where it would be assigned, either to the [priest's school] or to the [warrior's school], was as the mother, [and] as the father determined."

Our hypothetical family climbs into a canoe, and Tahtli paddles down one of the city's many canals. They float by willow trees, patios with blooming flowers, and other canoes passing back and forth like cars on a busy street.

Fray Bernardino de Sahagún, *Florentine Codex*, 16th century

Fray Bernardino de Sahagún, *Florentine Codex*, 16th century

When the family reaches the temple, they clamber out of the canoe and enter the building. The parents summon the old priests. One of the priests lifts the baby from Nantli's arms, holding her up as an offering to the god Quetzalcoatl. The well-behaved boys stand quietly while Nantli and Tahtli watch with pride.

"O master," the priest says, "here is thy vassal. . . . The mother, the father come bearing her. . . . Receive her. Perhaps for a little [while], she will perform for thee here the sweeping, the cleaning."

After the dedication is over, everyone celebrates with a feast. This is a joyful occasion, because the daughter's future is now secure. At the age of 15, she will return to this temple and begin her training as a priestess. Until then, she will live with her parents.

When the girl is three years old, Nantli will train her to be a polite and useful member of the family. It won't take long for the child to remember the rules of good behavior. If she is disrespectful or lazy, Nantli might stick her hand with a thorn.

Around the age of four, the daughter will learn the basics of weaving and spinning. That year she will also undergo a growth ritual. First, Nantli will pierce her earlobes and insert earrings, just as she did for her sons at that age. Then she will lift the girl by the forehead, stretching her body. Every year, Nantli pulls the nose, neck, ears, fingers, and legs of each of her children, believing that this will make their bodies grow strong and straight.

As infants, the three boys were dedicated at the temple,

Bernardino de Sahagún's manuscript, the Florentine Codex, *features native paintings of everyday Aztec items such as weaving tools. Women used the spindle whorls to spin thread and the battens to weave cloth.*

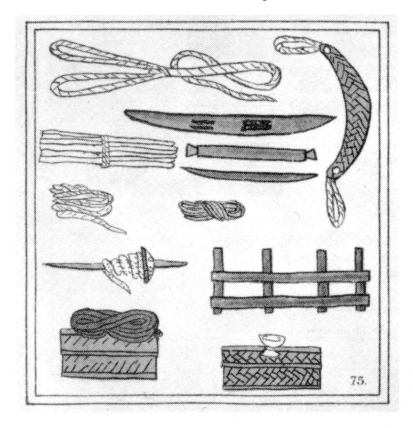

75.

too, so they know the paths they will follow in life. The oldest will attend a warrior school for boys called the House of Youths. The middle son will attend a preparatory school called the House of Song. The youngest will go to the strictest school of all—a kind of seminary that trains boys to become priests or government workers.

Parents in the Aztec Empire loved their children dearly, and showered them with attention and discipline. The children in this family would have learned to walk quickly with their heads held high. They spoke slowly in a soft voice and never stared at a woman, especially a married one. Gossip was forbidden. Most important, they learned the rules of eating: wash hands and face before each meal, avoid stuffing food in the mouth, and chew slowly (sound familiar?).

The years pass, and by 1499, the oldest son has completed training at the warrior school. During his first test battle, he captures a prisoner. As recognition for the deed,

In this illustration from the Codex Mendoza, a young man (left) carries gear, food, and other supplies for a veteran warrior (right). All young men in the Aztec Empire had to join the imperial army, either to learn the arts of war or to serve as porters for high-ranking warriors.

Women in Aztec Mexico had more rights than those in many cultures today. They carried their mother's surname through life. They could inherit land and property, and bring cases against women or men before the councils of justice. Women produced woven cloth, the most widely traded article in the empire—when the emperor wanted to honor one of his subjects with a gift, he gave him or her cloth that a woman had woven with gold thread. Women who died in childbirth were considered warriors who died in battle for the state. Their souls immediately went to the highest heaven.

his superiors shave the back of his head and paste feathers on it. The young man is relieved. If he had failed, the priests would have shaved only the crown of his head. Then the other young warriors would have called, "Big tuft of hair over the back of the head!" and he would have felt ashamed.

The middle son has just finished preparation at the House of Song. During the day, he learned farming techniques. At night, male priests taught him and other boys the sacred songs and dances that praise the gods. Now he will tend the family's plot of flowers in a *chinampa* outside the city.

The youngest boy is still undergoing rigorous training. The priests in his school have probably taught him to read large books with painted glyphs that tell the geography, myths, laws, and new history of Aztec society. The boy can name the stars and follow their passage through the sky. If he does something to offend the gods, he will go into the woods and bathe at midnight for penance. He might even fast for 24 hours without a scrap of food or a sip of water.

And now it is the daughter's turn. On her 15th birthday, she goes to the temple with Nantli and Tahtli. Here, a priestess addresses her. "Take heed, my daughter, my young noblewoman," the priestess says. "Enter there where the older sisters [priests] are all together. . . . Here is thy vow. Thou art to . . . take care of the sweeping, the cleaning. . . . Be diligent with the grinding stone, the chocolate, the making of offerings [for the gods]. And be obedient; do not be summoned twice."

Three years later, the daughter would be 18 years old. This is an important year for several reasons. First, she has fulfilled her parents' plans and is now a priestess who helps direct Aztec festivals and ceremonies. When she assists with the feast dedicated to the Mother Goddess, she paints herself white, sweeps the temple, and lights the fire. For the Great Feast of the Lords, she and her sister priests put on fringed cotton skirts embroidered with leaves or heart designs. Over these, they wear shifts with hanging streamers. The ribbons swirl gracefully around them as they dance, a sight made even more lovely when they unloose their braided hair.

"And when they danced, they unbound their hair; their hair just covered each one of them like a garment . . . "

Fray Bernardino de Sahagún, *Florentine Codex*, 16th century CE

All the Triple Alliance cities are lively places, and priestesses are an essential part of public celebrations. That's why the daughter might be present in Tenochtitlan for the greatest ceremony of 1502 CE: the inauguration of **Moctezuma II**, the new emperor.

In the past, Tenochtitlan, Texcoco, and Tlacopan had an equal vote in choosing a ruler. But Tenochtitlan is now the most powerful member of the Triple Alliance. Its nobles have decided on their own that Moctezuma will be the next emperor. Naturally, this doesn't go over well with the other cities. During the gala, the daughter might overhear ugly comments from the nobles from Texcoco and Tlacopan. They are disgusted by the amount of tribute they must give to Tenochtitlan. They even whisper that recent omens—comets in the sky, strange birds, and the eruption of a nearby volcano—signal the end of Tenochtitlan's greedy rule.

A few years later, the whispers turn to open debate when the king of Texcoco challenges Moctezuma to a rubber-ball game. He bets the emperor that the end of the Triple Alliance is near—that if he wins the ballgame, the victory will prove he is right. The two men play furiously, and the emperor loses. It's hard to believe that the city of flowers and song might disappear. But tragically, less than ten years later, the king's predictions will come true.

Moctezuma was the last emperor of the Aztec empire. A Spaniard who wrote about the Aztecs in the 16th century CE mistakenly spelled the emperor's name *Montezuma*. Modern Mexicans spell it *Moctezuma*.

Discovered in downtown Mexico City in 1790, this great stone is known as the Aztec Calendar Stone because a circular band of 20 hieroglyphs for the days of the sacred calendar surrounds the image of the Sun God.

CHAPTER 12

" BERNAL DÍAZ,
ALVA IXTILXOCHITL,
ANONYMOUS AZTEC
AUTHOR, AND
FRAY BERNARDINO
DE SAHAGÚN

WAR OF THE WORLDS
THE AZTEC ENCOUNTER THE SPANIARDS

conquistador = "conqueror" in
Spanish

" Bernal Díaz, *The True History
of the Conquest of New Spain*,
1584 CE

On November 6, 1519 CE, an army of 400 Spanish troops began the last leg of a long journey. Hernán Cortés, a Spanish **conquistador**, led the men. Their path lay straight ahead, between two volcanoes. "Sleeping Lady," a quiet volcano that behaved itself, was on the right. "Smoking Mountain," a monster that coughed hot steam, rose on the left.

Many of the soldiers sported full suits of metal armor. Sixteen of them rode horses, while the rest walked. Each man carried a lance, crossbow, musket, or shield. They marched in perfect formation, alert to danger, because this was unexplored Aztec territory. No one knew what waited beyond those volcanoes.

Years later, in 1584 CE, a Spanish foot soldier named Bernal Díaz described the march in a book that he called *The True History of the Conquest of New Spain*. "We began to climb the mountain with the greatest caution. . . . As we came to the top it began to snow, and the snow caked on the ground. We then marched down the pass."

More than 6,000 native warriors and porters followed the Spaniards. Seven enslaved native women traveled with them, too. Six were cooks brought along to cook tortillas for the army. The seventh was a 19-year-old with a gift for languages.

Young Malintzin had been born on the day One Twisted Grass, the unluckiest day in the sacred Aztec calendar. And, indeed, so far she had led an ill-fated life. Sold into slavery by her mother, she had been passed from one native group to another.

Malintzin was unlucky, but she was also smart. She already knew two native languages when a tribe gave her to

Cortés as a gift. She quickly learned Spanish and became his translator. The position finally gave Malintzin some control over her fate. Her life was at risk, but if she did her job well, she might escape a life of slavery.

The entire group was anxious for the journey to end. Six weeks earlier, they had left the turquoise waters of the Gulf Coast. Their destination was Tenochtitlan, the capital city of the Aztec empire. Their prize was control of the empire and its ruler, Moctezuma. The Spaniards hoped for extra bonuses, too: converting all the native people to Christianity and acquiring gleaming gold for themselves.

Hungry for riches, Cortés and his army headed inland through steaming lowlands. Beyond those jungles lay snow-covered peaks. While crossing the mountains, the travelers shivered in bitter winds and hunched their shoulders against rain and hail. Ravenous and cold, they finally descended onto a flat plain.

As they trekked west, the army encountered hostile native people who distrusted the Spaniards' clanking metal armor. Luckily for Cortés, though, these Mesoamericans were also sick of giving Moctezuma their precious gold, embroidered cloth, and feathers as tribute. Through force and persuasion, Cortés convinced them to become his allies. Only with their support could he dethrone the Aztec emperor.

But first Cortés had to enter the capital city. Would Moctezuma welcome him? It was hard to tell. As the army advanced, runners from Tenochtitlan arrived to meet

THE WOMAN WITH SEVEN NAMES

Before the conquest, Cortés gave Malintzin the baptismal name Marina. During the conquest, he gave her the title of Doña Marina, which is Spanish for Lady Marina. Someone, probably a Native American, nicknamed her Tapenal. The native word means "through the one who speaks."

After the conquest, Native Americans saw Malintzin as a villain who had helped the enemy. They dubbed her la lengua, which means "the tongue" in Spanish. Over time, "Malintzin" turned into "La Malinche," a combination of native and Spanish pronunciations. For a long while in Mexico, the word "malinche" stood for "traitor." Now many people think of her as a woman who used her intelligence and skills to survive slavery. They simply call her Malintzin.

Popocatepetl, or Smoking Mountain, lives up to its name in this photograph. Ash and cinders spewed from the volcano as Cortés and his men marched toward Mexico. Native people watching the eruption thought it was a bad omen.

them. The first group brought gold and silver as peace offerings. More runners announced that Moctezuma forbade entry into the city. Still more runners said Moctezuma would give the army food and lodging when it arrived.

What was Moctezuma really thinking? Cortés had no idea. And so, on the morning of November 8, 1519, his nervous army entered the Valley of Mexico. Tenochtitlan lay just ten miles ahead. The Spaniards were overwhelmed by the city in front of them, because it seemed to float on water.

Raised roads led to the sacred precinct, the Great Temple, and other important buildings in the center of Tenochtitlan. Hernán Cortés sent this map of the city to the king of Spain in 1524 to explain how it was that he defeated the great city. His invasion routes along the roads or causeways were a key part of the story.

On man-made islands, the Mexica had built a city almost three times larger than any in Spain, and much cleaner than any city in all of Europe. Mist from the water swirled around 60,000 buildings made of reeds, red volcanic rock, or white-painted adobe. Here and there, flat-topped pyramids with steep steps towered into the air.

An artificial land bridge led directly into the city. With the fearless Malintzin in front of him, the conquistador started across the bridge. Meanwhile, Moctezuma approached in grand fashion from the other side. Servants carried him on a litter, or platform, covered by a cloth awning. Residents of the city crowded the land bridge, while others gaped from canoes in the water. All had come to watch the great encounter between their emperor and the Spaniards. Would Moctezuma welcome the

"*A*nd when we saw all those cities and villages built in the water, and other great towns on dry land, and that straight and level causeway leading to Mexico [Tenochtitlan], we were astounded. These great towns and *cues* [pyramids] and buildings rising from the water, all made of stone, seemed like an enchanted vision. . . . Indeed, some of our soldiers asked whether it was not all a dream. . . . It was all so wonderful that I do not know how to describe this first glimpse of things never heard of, seen, or dreamed of before."

Bernal Díaz, *The True History of the Conquest of New Spain*, 1584 CE

Spaniards? Or had he arranged a surprise attack? The answer was . . . neither.

Moctezuma just could not make up his mind about Cortés. Perhaps the odd-looking man with pale skin and a long beard was an enemy. Or maybe he was a priest in the service of Topiltzin Quetzalcoatl (TQ), the Feathered Serpent god. After all, legend said this priest had sailed off across the eastern sea on a raft of serpents. Didn't the legend also say the priest would come back one day and restore his rightful rule? And didn't it say he would return from the eastern sea? Most important, the legend said that TQ would return in the Aztec year of One Reed. This was another stroke of luck for Cortés. The year 1519 happened to be the year One Reed.

Moctezuma already knew that Cortés had arrived from the eastern sea. Just in case he *was* TQ, the emperor gave the Spaniards a warm welcome. He led them to comfortable lodging in large houses, and he made sure they ate well. Grateful for a chance to relax, the soldiers enjoyed the pleasures of Tenochtitlan. They strolled through raised gardens, gawked at the pyramids, and wandered through the great marketplace.

Merchants from all over Mesoamerica displayed their goods in this market. Everything was for sale: slaves, pottery, honey cakes, jaguar skins, and human excrement used to age the skins and fertilize gardens. But even the amazing market couldn't distract Cortés from his task—theft of an empire.

Within a week of entering the city, the conquistador tricked Moctezuma with silky words and took him as prisoner. Malintzin was key to the bloodless capture. "Lord Moctezuma," she warned the king, "I advise you to accompany them [the Spaniards] to their quarters and make no protest. . . . If you stay here, you will be a dead man."

For all his treachery, Cortés was a polite jailer. He allowed Moctezuma to have visitors, and the prisoner enjoyed his usual royal comforts: servants, daily baths, and his cold chocolate drink. Cortés even played friendly games of catch with Moctezuma. And when a Spanish guard passed

Bernal Díaz, *The True History of the Conquest of New Spain*, 1584 CE gas within hearing of the royal ears, Cortés apologized for his soldier's coarse behavior.

Still, gold was gold. Cortés knew very well that he only had to give Charles, King of Spain, one-fifth of whatever treasures he found in the Americas. He also knew that Moctezuma was unaware of this fact. After holding the Aztec emperor prisoner for nine months, Cortés insisted that Moctezuma turn over his entire fortune as tribute to the Spanish king. Afraid for his life, Moctezuma agreed.

The Spaniards melted down precious ornaments and slabs of gold until they had almost 18,000 pounds. Cortés set aside a fifth of it for Charles I. Then the honey-mouthed conquistador talked his soldiers out of most of the rest. As far as we know, Malintzin received none.

What happened next depends on who wrote the history. According to Bernal Díaz, the native people thought Moctezuma had betrayed them. Disgusted, an angry crowd of warriors gathered in protest. Cortés was anxious to leave the city without violence, so he asked Moctezuma to calm the mob from a rooftop. The emperor agreed, but while he spoke, the people threw stones at him. Three of the missiles wounded him in the head, and he died within days.

But Alva Ixtilxochitl, an Aztec historian, wrote that "the Spaniards put him [Moctezuma] to death by stabbing him in the abdomen with their swords."

Alva Ixtilxochitl, *XIII relación*, 1608 CE

This elaborate chest ornament, or pectoral, is one of the finest examples of inlaid turquoise sculpture from ancient Mesoamerica. The double-headed serpent was a key symbol of rulership, and was tied to the Feathered Serpent (Quetzalcoatl) god who was the patron of Aztec priests and rulers.

Speech scrolls emerge from Moctezuma's mouth in this illustration from the Florentine Codex. He uses his best flowery words to try to persuade his people to disarm after the Spanish upset them by killing their people in an annual religious festival. The warriors below (bearing a shield with a battle symbol) would not heed his advice, and the Spaniards subsequently fled the city under cover of night.

66 Unknown Aztec author, *Unos anales históricos de la nación mexicana*, 1584 CE

66 Bernal Díaz, *The True History of the Conquest of New Spain*, 1584 CE

Either way, the game was up for the Spaniards. On June 30, 1520, they fled the city, weighed down with all the gold they could carry. In 1584, one Aztec described the scene: "The Spaniards attempted to slip out of the city at night, but we attacked furiously at the Canal of the Toltecs, and many of them died." Bernal Díaz later called this the "Night of Sorrow," estimating that one-third of the Spanish army lost their lives.

Aztec people died that night, too. According to Bernardino de Sahagún's scribes, "the warriors loosed a storm of arrows at the fleeing army. But the Spaniards also turned to

> *"We have pounded our hands in despair against the adobe walls, for our inheritance, our city, is lost and dead."*
>
> Anonymous Aztec scribe,
> from a poem about the fall of Tenotchitlan,
> written in 1528 CE

shoot at the Aztecs; they fired their crossbows. . . . The Spaniards . . . suffered many casualties, but many of the Aztec warriors were also killed or wounded."

Cortés and his army escaped to the Mexican countryside, where they built 30 flat-bottomed boats. Meanwhile, thousands of native people were dying because they had no immunity to the smallpox disease that Spanish soldiers had brought from Europe. Cortés returned to the death-ridden city in August of 1521. He brought the boats, his remaining Spanish army, and more native allies.

As the boats glided through the city, Cortés and his men set fire to buildings. The manned boats also kept food and fresh water from coming into the city, and its residents from going out. For three months, the trapped people starved. By the time the siege was over, Tenochtitlan lay in ruins, and at least 100,000 native people were dead.

Cortés had accomplished everything he set out to do. He now possessed a fabulous amount of gold: 10 million dollars in United States money today. The Aztec empire was now New Spain, and Spanish priests built a Christian church on top of a ruined pyramid.

And Malintzin? Still a slave, she bore Cortés a son. He was among the first mestizo, or mixed-blood, children born in the Americas. Later she married a Spanish lieutenant, and Cortés attended the wedding. As a gift, he presented her with an estate—land that used to belong to the Aztec Empire but was now his to give away.

In the war between the Spanish and Aztec worlds, the Spaniards had won. But victory would have been impossible without smallpox, luck, and native allies who had helped throughout the campaign. Above all, Malintzin had been necessary for Spanish success. As Díaz wrote, she was "the great beginning of our conquests."

THE SPOTTED CURSE

Smallpox is a contagious disease caused by a virus that comes from European cattle. For centuries, it was the curse of Europe, including Spain. Spaniards who conquered Mexico brought the disease with them unknowingly. They had already been exposed to smallpox in Spain, so their bodies had some resistance to the disease. Until the Spaniards came, smallpox and influenza were unknown in the Americas, so people there had no resistance. Within 100 years after the Spaniards arrived, smallpox and influenza had killed about 85 to 90 percent of the native population.

Smallpox symptoms include high fever, vomiting, and a rash that starts as small red spots. The rash turns into blisters. If a victim survives this dangerous phase of the illness, the sores scab over. Then the scabs fall off, often leaving a scar. There is no cure for smallpox, but a vaccine will prevent it. The last case of smallpox occurred in Somalia, Africa, in 1977.

CHAPTER 13

WAR OF THE WORLDS, CONTINUED

THE INCA AND THE SPANIARDS IN SOUTH AMERICA

huayna capac = "excellent youth" in Quechua

The powerful Inca emperor **Huayna Capac** had every reason to stand tall and proud in his litter. In 1493, he had become ruler of the Inca Empire. This vast territory covered 3,500 square miles. Stretching up and down the Andes Mountains of South America, it included deserts to the west and rainforests in the east. To the Inca, this was the Land of the Four Quarters. And Cuzco, the capital city, was the navel of the Inca world.

Eleven thousand feet high in the mountains of Peru, Cuzco was home to Inti, the Inca god of the sun. In his honor, the Inca built a temple with gold-plated walls. Outside the temple were broad avenues, flowing fountains, and walls of rock streaked with gold. What emperor wouldn't stand proudly when carried through such a city?

The mighty Inca emperor Huayna Capac holds a shield and swings a sling as servants carry him in his war litter. A fearsome and successful warrior, Huayna Capac could not have imagined the fate that befell him, his heirs, and the empire after the Spaniards invaded.

Huayna Capac was proud of his many sons, too. **Atahualpa**, a handsome man, lived in the city of Quito, in present-day Ecuador. From there, he governed the northern section of the empire with an iron hand. His half brother, **Huascar Inca**, lived in Cuzco and was confident he would inherit his father's crown. Apparently, Huascar Inca was nothing like his name. Between 1567 and 1615, an Inca named Guamán Poma wrote in Spanish an illustrated history of the Inca. It describes Huascar as "long-faced, graceless and ugly, with an unpleasant character."

{ *atahualpa* = "wild turkey cock" in Quechua

{ *huascar inca* = "gentle hummingbird" in Quechua

Beginning in 1524, two forces were about to change this family and their empire forever. Huayna Capac was in Quito when he heard that light-skinned bearded men in floating fortresses had landed on the coast of present-day Panama.

Huayna Capac also heard that an invisible enemy—smallpox—was running wild through the northern part of his empire. As the smallpox virus made its way south, so did the bearded men in floating fortresses. By 1526, the strangers were snooping around the coast of northern Peru, dangerously close to the empire. Francisco Pizarro, a Spanish conquistador and cousin of Hernán Cortés, was captain of the sailing expedition.

Guamán Poma describes what happened when one of Pizarro's men went ashore. An Inca noble greeted the Spanish soldier and asked what he ate; the Spaniard answered that he "lived on silver and gold. The Inca thereupon gave him some silver and gold-dust and a quantity of gold plate."

66 Guamán Poma, *Letters to a King,* 1567

Runners reported the Spaniard's puzzling appetite to Huayna Capac, but before he could react, smallpox struck him down in 1527. Guamán Poma writes that Huayna Capac "fled from human company and hid in a rocky cave where he spent his last hours alone." Unfortunately, the king had never named a successor. Soon after his remains arrived in Cuzco, civil war broke out.

The royal court in Cuzco declared Huascar Inca emperor of the Land of the Four Quarters. Atahualpa, still in Quito, was incensed. Hadn't he proven himself in battle? Hadn't he helped his father govern Quito? *He* should rule

66 Guamán Poma, *Letters to a King,* 1567

The last Inca emperor, Atahualpa, wears the headdress and large earrings that symbolize his high office.

ATAHUALLPA, INCA XIIII.

the northern part of the empire, while his worthless brother could rule the lands from Cuzco south to Chile.

A deadly game of seesaw began. Huascar Inca expected his brother to visit Cuzco and bow and scrape, but Atahualpa wouldn't budge. Furious, Huascar Inca ordered his men to capture Atahualpa. They did, but the prisoner escaped, and in turn, his troops captured Huascar Inca. Atahualpa executed Huascar Inca's family in front of his eyes, then threw him in prison. Disease, death, feuding brothers—the Inca Empire was a disaster by 1532.

Pizarro and his paltry army of 260 men were still lurking on the coast of Peru. Pizarro knew that the empire had no official ruler and was in chaos. Then he heard that Atahualpa was in Cajamarca, a mere two-week march away. It was time to close in for the kill.

The conquistador and his men began the treacherous ascent into the Andes. The mountains were so steep that the men climbed off their horses, carefully leading them up narrow paths that overlooked deep gorges. One misstep, and man or beast could hurtle thousands of feet down through the air. The venture was reckless, but Pizarro was suffering from what Cortés called a "disease of the heart that can only be cured by gold."

Runners informed Atahualpa that bearded ones were approaching Cajamarca. Guamán Poma described what the messengers saw. "The [Spanish] men looked as if they were shrouded liked corpses," he wrote. Their faces "were cov-

Bernal Díaz, *The True History of the Conquest of New Spain*, 1584

Guamán Poma, *Letters to a King*, 1567

ered with wool, leaving only the eyes visible," and their caps "resembled little red pots on top of their heads."

The Spaniards probably looked like walking dead to the Inca. But the strangers were few in number, so the runners quickly returned to Cajamarca, assuring Atahualpa there was nothing to fear. Still, residents of the town must have thought that aliens had arrived when the Spaniards appeared on November 15, 1532. Plumes on their helmets waved in the breeze, and saddle bells jingled as their horses pranced through the streets. The Inca were used to leading around petite llamas that carried loads for them. But

INCA EMPIRE AT ITS GREATEST EXTENT, 1525 CE

Inca Empire

Quito

Caxamarca

Pacific Ocean

Cuzco

Andes Mountains

ECUADOR

PERU

BRAZIL

CHILE

UNDELIVERED MAIL

Guamán Poma was born in Peru just after the Spanish conquest. He grew up during the very years when Inca customs were disappearing under Spanish rule. The loss saddened and angered him, so at age 32 he began a 1200-page letter to the king of Spain. Divided into three parts, the letter described how the Spaniards were mistreating his people. It also explained the lost traditions his elders remembered from pre-Spanish days. The letter, which is now kept in the Royal Library of Copenhagen, Denmark, is illustrated with almost 400 simple drawings.

By age 89, Guamán Poma was still writing the letter. He finally sent it off to Madrid, the capital of Spain, in 1615. But scholars think it fell into the hands of a Danish official, and the king never read it. Guamán Poma's letter is the most accurate colonial chronicle—text written after the Spaniards arrived—that we have of life in the Inca Empire.

Francisco Pizarro heard from Hernán Cortés how he had captured the Aztec emperor Moctezuma and conquered his empire. Pizarro took a page out of Cortés's playbook and successfully conquered the Inca empire, only to be killed by one of his own soldiers a year later after an argument about who should control part of the conquered territories.

66 Guamán Poma, *Letters to a King,* 1567

they had never seen a beast big enough to ride and thought horses were giant human beings.

Pizarro had learned a trick or two about conquests from Cortés: soften the enemy with lies, then pounce. He sent another conquistador, Hernando de Soto, in search of Atahualpa. De Soto rode a few miles out to the town's hot springs. Here he found the ruler soaking in a pool fed by two pipes of water—one cold, one hot—and surrounded by his chiefs.

Guamán Poma writes that de Soto nudged his horse with his thighs, and the obedient creature made a "sudden charge toward the imperial party. The sound of bells and the hoof-beats produced the utmost consternation." Atahualpa remained calm, but his men "fled in terror at the sight of the huge animals and riders."

Then the lies began. De Soto bragged that the Spaniards were skilled fighters, and that Pizarro could help Atahualpa become emperor. Historians don't know if the bluff worked or not. Did Atahualpa really believe that Pizarro would be his ally? Or did Atahualpa just pretend to believe the lie? Whatever the reason, the Inca ruler agreed to meet Pizarro in town the following day.

That night, Pizarro's men camped in the center of Cajamarca, while the Inca camped on hillsides that surrounded the valley town. The Spaniards could see light flickering from thousands of Inca campfires. Knowing they were wildly outnumbered, some of the soldiers were so frightened that they "made water without knowing it." Atahualpa, meanwhile, planned on leaving 80,000 troops in the countryside and taking 5,000 troops to the meeting.

The following day, Atahualpa kept the nervous Spaniards waiting until sunset. Finally the ruler arrived, held aloft on a wooden litter decorated with jewels, silver, and gold. He carried a gold shield engraved with a picture of the sun. A lone Spanish friar was waiting as the procession entered the town square.

Spanish law stated that conquistadors must give native people the chance to accept Christianity before blood was shed. So the friar held a cross in one hand and a prayer book in the other. When he tried to convince Atahualpa to accept the Christian god, the Inca scoffed. "You say your god was put to death," he replied through a translator, "but my god still lives," and he pointed to the sun.

Atahualpa's refusal to accept Christianity was all Pizarro needed to justify the slaughter that followed. Hidden until

66 Bernal Díaz, *The True History of the Conquest of New Spain,* 1584

The conquistador Francisco Pizarro (seated, left) orders the assassination of the Inca emperor, Atahualpa, after a hasty trial. Atahualpa had been falsely accused of treason against Pizarro by a Spanish soldier who had made advances on Atahualpa's wife. The soldier who accused him was later exposed as a liar, but by then Atahualpa was dead.

EARLIER, IN NORTH AMERICA

In 100 CE, the Anasazi Indians were living in the Four Corners region, where Utah, Arizona, New Mexico, and Colorado meet. The Anasazi mummified their dead and gave them sandals for life in the afterworld.

now, the Spaniards stormed out of a building and fired off two cannons. Waving their steel swords, they sliced off the hands of the 80 men carrying Atahualpa's huge litter.

Pizarro dragged the ruler through a doorway and placed him under guard. Over the next two hours, the conquistador and his few men massacred 5,000 stunned Inca warriors. Not one Spaniard died, because Atahualpa had made a terrible blunder: astonishingly, none of his men was armed. The mistake is understandable, because the Spaniards had broken the rules of warfare as Atahualpa knew them. In the ancient Americas, warriors didn't claim to come in peace and then attack.

Pizarro imprisoned Atahualpa for the next 20 days. The ruler made the best of it. He learned to speak and read Spanish; he played chess with the guards and won, to their dismay. Determined that Huascar Inca would never take his place, he also sent secret orders to supporters in Cuzco: his brother must be killed and the body cut to pieces.

Atahualpa knew that the Spaniards lusted for silver and gold. In exchange for freedom, he offered to fill his entire cell, as far as he could reach above his head, with gold and silver ornaments. The room was 22 feet by 17 feet—no wonder Pizarro eagerly agreed. On orders from Atahualpa, the Inca began sending finely carved sculptures from Cuzco. The Spaniards melted the pieces into 13,400 pounds of gold and 26,000 pounds of silver. Then Pizarro's advisors convinced him that they should burn Atahualpa at the stake.

> *"When Atahualpa died, all the Indians gathered there in Cajamarca returned to their lands, and the roads were full of them as if they were rows of ants."*
>
> Juan de Betanzos,
> *Narrative of the Incas,* 1550s

The Inca ruler despaired when he heard the news. Unless his people could mummify his body, his soul would die, too. The Spaniards agreed to strangle Atahualpa instead if he would convert to Christianity. He agreed at the last minute. What happened after the Spaniards strangled him is unclear. One story says the body disappeared. But Spanish writer Pedro de Cieza de León wrote in 1552 that the Spaniards "burned some of his [Atahualpa's] hair," then buried him.

Whatever happened to Atahualpa, his last breath marked the end of the Inca Empire. Manco Capac, one of Huayna Capac's other sons, established a city hidden deep in the Peruvian rainforests on the eastern slopes of the Andes Mountains. Over the next 35 years, he, his sons, and their loyal followers left the hideaway periodically to raid Spanish settlements. But every attempt at reclaiming the empire failed. All the Inca land, silver, and gold now belonged to Spain.

66 Pedro de Cieza de León, *The Discovery and Conquest of Peru*, 1552

Keros, or painted wooden drinking cups, were very popular in pre-Columbian times, so much so that they continued to be made after European contact. The colonial period keros have elaborate scenes of people and daily life. This one has European figures and a portrait of an African-Peruvian on the top, with typical cats on the bottom.

LUGGING LLAMAS

Ancient Andeans used llamas as pack animals, but they also ate dried llama meat and wove llama wool into cloth. Andean highlanders still use llamas for lugging loads of food, tools, and water. Some North Americans now raise the animals, too. Usually friendly and gentle, llamas make good pets. They're also handy for carrying camping gear on a long hike, because their soft hooves don't damage wilderness trails.

Llamas can make a symphony of different sounds. Mama llamas and their babies hum to each other. Both males and females give warning calls if they sense danger. Sometimes males snort at each other, trying to prove which one is boss. When a fight develops, their screams sound like squealing pigs.

CHAPTER 14

" PEDRO DE CIEZA
DE LEÓN

ROLLER-COASTER ROADS
UP AND DOWN
THE ANDEAN WORLD

What were Pedro's parents *thinking*? Their son was only 12 years old—much too young to leave Seville, in southwestern Spain, and travel across the wide Atlantic Ocean. But Pedro de Cieza de León was determined to go, and with good reason. An educated boy, he had read ancient

THE ANDEAN WORLD

Mesoamerica includes all of central and southern Mexico, Guatemala, Belize, El Salvador, and parts of Honduras. The Andean world stretches along either side of the Andes Mountains in South America. It includes present-day Peru and Ecuador, and parts of Bolivia, Chile, and Argentina.

THE ANDES

Greek and Roman histories and traveled through Spain with his merchant father. Yet nothing could compare with the glittering riches he saw on January 9, 1534.

A Spanish ship sailed into the harbor of Seville that day. Like everyone else in town, Pedro gaped when soldiers unloaded gold worth millions of Spanish pesos, and silver ingots the size of bricks. Two years earlier, the Spanish conquistador Franciso Pizarro had conquered the Inca Empire and claimed its riches for the king of Spain. Now his ship had returned home, packed with the spoils of war. Pedro wanted to see for himself the continent that could produce such wealth.

Perhaps the boy pestered his mother and father until they gave in. Or maybe they thought their son could handle a great adventure on his own. However it happened, Pedro's parents arranged the trip for him. He was barely 13 years old when the captain of another Spanish ship agreed to let him come aboard, probably as a serving boy. In March 1535, the captain and his crew left Seville with two goals. They hoped to discover the passage to India that Christopher Columbus had never found. And they wanted piles and piles of gold.

Two months later, the vessel landed on the northern coast of present-day Colombia, South America. The men poled south up a river, searching for the passage. But after reaching a dead end, the crew switched to horseback. While riding overland with the men, Pedro kept a mental diary of everything he saw. Six years later, in 1541, he turned a drum into a table and whittled a quill pen from the feather of a **condor**. Then he started writing a book he would call *Chronicle of Peru*.

Other Europeans recorded their impressions of the Americas after the Spanish conquest. But curious Pedro was one of the few who tried to describe South American people and customs without judging them. The young author began by remembering native people he had seen shortly after arriving in the Americas. They "lived in small villages, in houses like long sheds, sleeping in hammocks . . . they are clean in their eating . . . the lords are obeyed and feared

A condor is a large Andean vulture.

Pedro de Cieza de León, *Chronicle of Peru*, 1547

. . . and their women are the prettiest and most lovable of any that I have seen in the Indies."

Pedro Cieza de León was 27 when he left Colombia and headed south into the old Inca Empire. Take a roller-coaster ride with him now as he explores this up-and-down world.

After crossing into what is now northern Ecuador, Cieza de León rode south along a rugged range of the Andes Mountains. Land along the 10,000-foot-high mountain road was "rough and barren," he wrote in his book. Despite the terrain, people had built lodgings and storehouses along the way. For Cieza de León, a highway built despite such difficulties was "an astounding thing to see."

As the young man continued south, the road dipped into fertile valleys fed by warm rivers, then rose again to desolate mountain highlands. When he reached Quito, in present-day Ecuador, he rode down once more, deep into a hollow ringed by mountains.

Cieza de León marveled at the strange foods he saw in Quito: potatoes, which he wrote were "as soft inside as boiled chestnuts," and quinoa, a plant with edible seeds that "grows almost to a man's height . . . and which they also eat boiled, as we do rice." Stranger still were the great flocks of animals that the Spaniards, lacking a better name, called sheep: two-toed llamas, wooly alpacas, and deer-like vicuña.

In 1548, Cieza de León left the valleys of Ecuador. He descended on a road that linked the mountains with the dry coastal deserts of Peru. In his book, he described the flip-flopping weather as he passed from one altitude to another. "One can come down to the plains wearing a rain cape which is soaking wet," he wrote, "and before nightfall find oneself in regions where . . . it has never rained."

The coastal desert was a barren, windy land where only thistles and thorns grew. In some areas, there was nothing but sand. No wonder Cieza de León went back up to the Andes! This time, he took a different connector road—a breathtaking stone highway built into the solid-rock wall of a river canyon. The road swooped to an altitude of 16,000 feet, then plunged into a valley.

Pedro de Cieza de León,
Chronicle of Peru, 1547

Pedro de Cieza de León,
Chronicle of Peru, 1547

ONE POTATO, TWO POTATO . . .

We store potatoes and other root crops exactly the way that ancient people stored them: in a cool, dry spot. For us, that spot might be a root cellar, or basement. For ancient highlanders, it was a ware-house. Raw maize keeps well in the cool, dry high-lands, too.

Even though Cieza de León was a first-rate writer, he found himself unable to describe the scenery adequately. He could only explain how he felt after climbing one of the highest peaks. "I was so done in that it was very difficult for me to reach the top," he wrote, "and on turning to gaze down, it seemed that the ravines reached down into the bowels of hell."

66 Pedro de Cieza de León, *Chronicle of Peru*, 1547

In 1549, Cieza de León made his way to Lake Titicaca, the highest lake in the world. Then he went to the southeastern side of the lake. By now, he and his horse were lugging around 8,000 handwritten pages of text. He still hadn't seen the Amazon River that curled through rainforests east of the Andes, but his horse couldn't carry the weight of any more journals. It was time to leave South America. By 1550, Cieza de León was back in Seville, home again after 3,000 miles and 16 years of travel.

Cieza de León's chronicle was more than a record of the geography of the Inca Empire. His account left a trail of clues scholars now use when figuring out how the Inca accomplished so much in less than 100 years.

The Inca improved a system of up-and-down living that Andean people had invented thousands of years earlier. The

The snow-capped Andes Mountains tower above fertile river valleys below. Melting snow flows down into rivers that irrigate fields on the coastal deserts of South America.

Lake Titicaca is the highest major lake on earth. By creating raised fields in shallow waters at the lake's edge, ancient highland farmers prevented damage to their crops from night frosts, since bodies of water always cut down on temperature extremes.

system worked like this: When people first settled in the Andes Mountains, many of them ended up on high, flat plains called *puna*. It was a good choice, because flat land meant more farmland. Unfortunately, only a few kinds of food, such as potatoes and quinoa, grew in the cold, dry highlands. If long droughts or cold spells destroyed the harvest, there was little else to eat.

Just as Mesoamericans learned to live with droughts and floods, ancient Andeans learned to make the most of their up-and-down geography. They did it partly by organizing themselves into groups of families called *ayllus*. These families weren't related, but they were close-knit and helped one another. And eventually they figured out how to keep from starving.

When food was scarce, the leader of an *ayllu* would send some families to lower altitudes, where people could raise different kinds of foods. Think of it as a giant staircase, with people living on different steps. Some families moved to the Pacific coast, or the bottom step. Here, they made small boats from reeds and caught huge amounts of seafood. The coastal deserts were bone dry, but people learned how to irrigate fields with water flowing down from the mountains. Then they raised maize, cotton, beans, and squash.

Ayllu leaders also sent families to Lake Titicaca, where they made raised beds of soil along the edge of the lake. Then they planted crops on top and let lake water run into furrows between the fields. Still others moved to thick rainforests on the eastern side of the Andes, where they harvested **manioc** root. No matter where the families moved, they were still members of their original highland community.

The word *manioc* comes from *manioka*, the word of the South American Tupi people for a shrub that grows in the tropics. The root can grow to about the size of a rolled-up newspaper, and people cook it like potatoes and use it to make a starch called tapioca. If you've eaten tapioca pudding, you've had food made from manioc.

Llamas were the beasts of burden that made it possible for Andean civilizations to ship goods up and down the mountains and along their roller-coaster roads. They were loved, and even worshipped, sometimes playing prominent parts in religious rites and festivals. This beautiful example of a silver llama shows the quality of Inca silversmithing as well as the deep affection that people had for these animals.

A collqa, *or storage facility, one of thousands of storehouses for goods built throughout the Inca empire. Many of these stored supplies for the imperial army, including food, clothing, and weapons. Others were used to store surplus local goods so they could be shipped to other parts of the empire.*

When harvests at any of the different levels were good, people stored extra food in warehouses they built along trails. These trails led from the flat coast up over the Andes and down into the rainforests. A member of the *ayllu* was left in charge of each warehouse. If lack of rain meant a low harvest at one altitude, hungry colonists roped their llamas together in a caravan, traveled to a storehouse at another elevation, and helped themselves.

Llama trains also hauled other goods like cloth, cotton, and pottery. Only the llamas interfered with this efficient system. If a load weighs more than about 100 pounds, the animals spit in protest and refuse to budge.

Inca emperors knew a good thing when they saw it. After forcing various *ayllus* to join the empire in 1438, they improved the ancient trails into the roller-coaster roads that astonished Cieza de León.

CHAPTER 15

A TALE OF TWO CITIES

THE OLDEST TOWNS IN THE AMERICAS

If you like adventure travel, you might enjoy a tour of the oldest towns in the Americas. The trip won't be easy, though. First, you'll fly to Lima, Peru, a modern coastal city that Francisco Pizarro founded in 1535. Then you'll hire a guide who knows the area. He'll drive you north in a four-wheel-drive vehicle, following the Pan American Highway that hugs the Peruvian coastline. After 115 miles, he'll turn off the highway and head east on a gravel road.

About 17 bumpy miles later, you'll reach a long sandy beach. Here is the site of an ancient coastal settlement called Aspero. This amazing place covers 37 acres, with 17 flat-topped mounds in the center. The mounds range in height from 13 to 32 feet. They were built around 2857 and 2558 BCE.

" Mounds of Aspero, Peru, 2587 and 2558 BCE

In the 1970s, archaeologists excavated two of these mounds and found a compartment near the top of one. Inside were the corpses of an adult and a two-month-old infant, each wrapped in cotton cloth. The archaeologists believe that an ancient ruler built this mound as proof of his power. And the bodies were probably offerings—sacrifices that the ruler made to honor the gods.

After exploring the mounds, the archaeologists started excavating in the ground. They were surprised when they didn't find evidence of corn, beans, squash, or any other planted crops. Instead, they discovered piles of bones and shells.

A WARPED IDEA

Spinning thread and making cloth are the oldest crafts in the Andean world. First, the spinner cleaned and combed a handful of raw cotton or wool. Then she placed it on top of a long stick called a drop spindle. The spindle was weighted at the end with a stone. As the spinner quickly rotated the stick, the weight of the stone gathered the fibers into long threads.

To weave cloth, ancient people used a technique called twining. First, the weaver laid out a set of vertical threads called warp threads. Using her fingers, she wove horizontal threads, or weft threads, under and over the warp. Sometimes she twisted the weft threads as she worked, or she tied a weft thread to a warp thread. By using threads of different colors, ancient weavers created images of eagles, snakes, and crabs.

Aspero's population ate seafood, and lots of it: mussels, clams, sardines, and especially anchovies.

This was unusual. Other civilizations in the world had developed around the same time as Aspero, but they began only when people planted crops and had a steady food supply. Mesoamerica is a good example of the birth of civilization—if it weren't for beans, maize, and squash, early Mesoamerican villages would never have grown into towns and cities. People in Aspero didn't know beans about raising beans or any other crops. Still, they managed to survive on seafood and build those gigantic mounds.

Most archaeologists call an ancient settlement a city if at least 10,000 people lived there. And those people would have had a variety of jobs, such as making tools or being warriors. The archaeologists digging at Aspero knew the site was very large, but was it a city? They weren't sure, because they didn't excavate the entire site.

Maybe Aspero was a ceremonial center. Such places became lively when crowds of visitors arrived to worship the gods. But most of the time, just a few people lived there, and the settlement was like a ghost town. Was this Aspero's story? The archaeologists had no idea.

Now your guide will leave Aspero, turn away from the sea, and drive up into the Supe Valley. The valley stretches southeast for 60 miles, mostly following the Supe River. Here is where the scenery will make your trip worthwhile, because the river winds between colossal Andean mountains that tower right and left. The sight is breathtaking.

During the slow, bouncy ride up the valley, you'll notice the sites of younger settlements that archaeologists have found along the river. Around 1800 BCE, ancient people walked about 12 miles inland from the coast and settled down. Now that they lived away from the coast, they couldn't catch fish, so they needed a different food supply. They built canals from the river to fields and raised squash, beans, and maize. They also built sunken round plazas from stone. These open areas were sacred gathering places where people left offerings as a kind of thank-you note to the gods for good harvests.

After the gravel road becomes a dirt track, you may pass Peruvian women herding goats and tending maize fields. You won't see modern conveniences, though, because the Supe Valley is a remote place with no electricity or running water. Finally, you'll reach the midpoint of the valley, 15 miles from the sea. By now, you'll be ready to clamber out of the four-wheel-drive and stretch your legs. And here is the perfect spot: a wide table of land that sits 82 feet above the Supe River. This windswept terrace is the site of ancient Caral.

In 1994, aerial photography revealed six mounds in Caral. The photographs intrigued Peruvian archaeologist Ruth Shady, so she visited the site. She was astounded. Shady had seen Aspero, but in all her years of surveying and digging, she had never seen anything that seemed as big as Caral.

❝ Mounds of Caral, Peru, 3000 BCE

For two years, Shady surveyed Caral. It covered 160 acres—more than four times the area of Aspero. Then she measured the largest mound. **Pirámide Mayor** was five stories high and the size of four football fields. By 1996, she was ready to explore this giant.

{ *pirámide mayor* = "great pyramid" in Spanish

Native people living nearby were curious. As Shady dug, they asked how their ancestors could have built such a huge thing. Five years later, she could answer the question. To build Pirámide Mayor, ancient people first cut rocks with stone tools. They piled up the rocks to make walls around the base of the pyramid. Next, they made small mesh bags from reeds and filled them with loose rubble. Step by step, bag by bag, the builders lugged more than

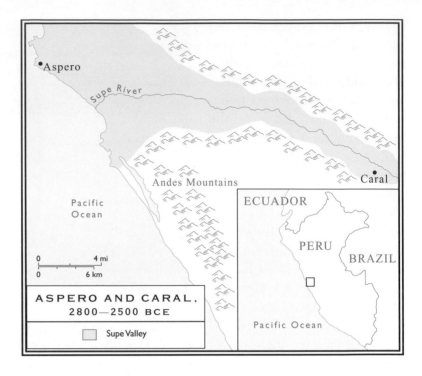

ASPERO AND CARAL,
2800—2500 BCE

Supe Valley

7 million cubic feet of rock and placed it inside the walls. After the builders filled in the mound, they carefully plastered the walls and painted them red. When radiocarbon dating proved that the mesh bags were made in 2750 BCE, Shady was excited. Pirámide Mayor isn't quite as old as Aspero's oldest mound. But it might be the oldest one in the Supe Valley, and archaeologists didn't think ancient people had moved inland so early.

Reed bags filled with rocks were used to build the huge mounds at Caral, Peru. Dry desert conditions kept the bags intact for over 4,000 years.

Five smaller mounds surround Pirámide Mayor. Near all six mounds, Shady and her team found apartment-style living quarters and household trash. The builders had used the same materials for these houses as they had for the pyramid walls: cut stone covered with heavy plaster. Beyond the center of the site, the excavators uncovered houses with smaller rooms and walls made from wooden poles, cane, and mud. Just as Egyptian construction workers lived near their pyramids, the workers who built the mounds at Caral may have lived in these structures.

Shady also uncovered two sunken plazas that could have held hundreds of people. When you rode through the Supe Valley on the way to Caral, you saw similar circular pits at the younger sites. Shady thinks people in these places played follow the leader—that Caral influenced their architecture and religion.

Other discoveries helped Shady understand why Caral was established in the first place. While digging, she and her co-workers found traces of ancient squash and beans

The circular amphitheater at Caral was lined with benches for high-status people who wanted to sit while watching ceremonies in the arena below.

A PARTY PIT

Droughts, floods, and earthquakes plagued the Andean world and still do. Ancient people believed that the gods controlled these forces of nature. So it was wise to keep the deities happy by performing ceremonies in their honor. People built sunken plazas where they could gather in one spot for festivals and feasts.

Some of the circular pits had two sets of steps on opposite sides. Archaeologists think that people formed a procession, entering by one staircase and leaving by the other. In one sunken plaza at Caral, Ruth Shady dug up 32 flutes made from condor and pelican bones, and 37 cornets made of deer and llama bones—signs that 5,000 years ago, people played music as they partied in honor of the gods.

and an irrigation canal that still runs below the site. These signs of agriculture were no surprise. Like people in the younger settlements of the Supe Valley, those in Caral built canals, irrigated their fields, and raised crops.

What amazed Shady were the remains of seafood. She found great quantities of clam and mussel shells, along with the bones of sardines and of that old standby, anchovies. How did so much seafood get to a place 14 miles from the ocean? The archaeologist also discovered traces of the achiote plant, which grows in tropical rainforests on the eastern side of the Andes Mountains. Caral is on the western side of the mountains. How did achiote get to Caral?

Most fascinating of all, Shady found large quantities of cottonseeds, cotton fibers, and cotton cloth in almost every building. What were the people of Caral doing with so much cotton?

Shady believes that at certain times of the year, fisherfolk from Aspero lugged baskets of seafood to Caral and left with baskets of cotton for weaving cloth. And at some point, a couple of pieces of that cloth ended up as burial shrouds for an adult and two-month-old child in one of Aspero's mounds.

Farmers from the rainforest traveled to Caral, too, and traded achiote for cotton. So Caral might be the earliest example of Andean people making the most of their up-and-down world. They lived on the coast or in the foothills, highlands, or forests, and they came together to share what grew best at home. The gatherings at Caral might have been the first potluck dinners in history.

But for Shady, Caral means much more. Six mounds spread over a large area, sunken plazas that could be older than any others in Peru—this evidence proves to her that Caral is the largest and oldest city in the Americas. And the remains of seafood and cotton show that it was a major trading center.

Not all archaeologists share Shady's conclusions about Caral. They agree that it might have been on a trade route, and that the two public gathering places are signs of an ancient religion. But does Caral qualify as a city? Maybe it was a ceremonial center. Nobody can know until the entire site has been excavated.

And archaeologists still don't know if Aspero was a city or a ceremonial center, either. Thirty years have passed since they first started excavating there. Digging up 37 acres is a lot of work, and Aspero and Caral are only two of hundreds of ancient settlements in Peru. There are too many sites, and not enough trained people to excavate them.

When archaeologists excavate all of Caral and Aspero, they'll be on the lookout for a large number of houses and many different kinds of tools: evidence that at least 10,000 people lived and worked in these places. Only then will they know the age, size, and purpose of the settlements. But don't ask, "Is that your final answer?" By that time, other archaeologists may have found an even older or bigger site in coastal Peru, and the discussion will start all over again.

Meanwhile, Shady is concerned about the ruins in Caral. Before you climb back into the four-wheel-drive vehicle, look around. You'll notice that rain, wind, and air pollution are destroying fragments of paint on walls, and structures are crumbling.

The corrosive pollution troubles Shady and her team. Yet even nagging worry can't dampen the pride and enthusiasm they feel for the special place they've uncovered. They hope Caral will help people in Peru remember that their history started long before the Spaniards arrived.

BUILDING UP, DIGGING DOWN

2857 BCE
Aspero people build first high mound

2750 BCE
Caral people build Pirámide Mayor and plazas

2558 BCE
Aspero people build second high mound

1800 BCE
Coastal people move inland, build plazas

1970s CE
Archaeologists partly excavate Aspero

1990s CE
Archaeologists partly excavate Caral

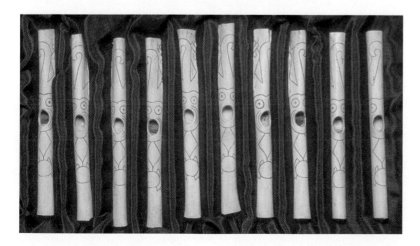

Archaeologists found these fancifully carved bone flutes while digging in the amphitheater at Caral. The Andean flute music of today is the latest version of musical traditions dating back thousands of years.

CHAPTER 16

THE THUNDEROUS TEMPLE
ANDEAN PEOPLE CONNECT

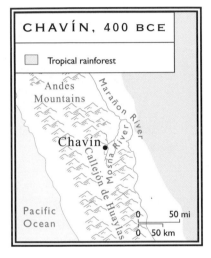

Tropical rainforest

Andes Mountains

Marañon River

Mosna River

Chavín

Callejón de Huaylas

Pacific Ocean

0   50 mi
0   50 km

Aspero and Caral may have been the first large towns to pop up on the Peruvian coast. But for the next 2,000 years, many others followed. Meanwhile, people in the highlands were settling down in cities, too. In northern Peru, in a mountain valley midway between the western coast and eastern rainforests, at a place where two rivers meet, stand the ruins of a town called Chavín de Huántar. Around 400 BCE, priests built a U-shaped temple in the middle of this settlement. Archaeologists who have explored the site believe that it was a major ceremonial center—a place of worship—in ancient times.

A walled circular pit that could hold 500 people sat in front of the temple. Pilgrims gathered here before entering the sacred place ahead, though none of them did it with a light heart. Monstrous stone heads twice the size of their own were attached midway up the plaza walls. Carved streams of mucus poured from the noses of the heads as they stared with bulging eyes at the crowd.

The main temple of Chavín de Huántar was built around 400 BCE. Surely the memory of this temple stuck with the thousands of pilgrims who came here from all parts of the civilized Andean world.

The heads were a warning of what was to come, but the visitors were ready. Archaeologists don't know if women pilgrims visited Chavín. But from studying colonial chronicles, they know that later male Andean pilgrims purified themselves before visiting a temple—they slept for a time without their wives, and they ate food without salt and chili peppers. Male pilgrims to Chavín probably fasted the same way.

Once pure, the pilgrims could approach the oracle inside the temple and ask questions about the future. Would they suffer from disease? Would rain and sunshine bless their crops the following year? Would an earthquake split the earth, swallowing their families and houses? Only the oracle knew. Represented by a statue deep within the heart of the temple, he was the god above all other gods.

To please the oracle, the pilgrims brought offerings of dried fish and maize. While they waited in the plaza with their gifts, a low rumble started in the temple, as if a mudslide or torrent of floodwater was gathering strength. The sound turned to a thunderous roar, then slowly subsided.

Scared witless by now, the visitors formed a solemn procession and walked up a center staircase leading to the open part of the U. At this point, they may have given the offerings to a priest, who then led them in groups of six to eight as they descended steps and entered the underground temple. Walking single-file, they wound through long, dark, windowless hallways and past mysterious chambers.

Torches could have lit these maze-like halls. Even so, the dim light may have confused the pilgrims and made them feel cut off from the world outside.

In one hallway, the pilgrims passed a woman's skull resting on a shelf. Eight hundred pots filled with dried deer and llama meat and dried fish were stored in another hallway. Archaeologists who excavated these jars think the contents may have been gifts from previous pilgrims. After passing a room that held hundreds of human bones, the pilgrims reached the belly of the temple: a chamber with a hole in the stone floor.

Heads of gods were once attached to the walls of the main temple at Chavín de Huántar. Ancient people believed that the heads were supernatural forces that lived in the temple and inside its walls.

EARLIER, IN GREECE

In 1200 BCE, people in the Mediterranean world visited the Oracle of Delphi in Greece. Ancient people believed that a priestess at this shrine could tell them when to plant seeds or go to war.

The Lanzón sculpture, Chavín de Huántar, 400 BCE

A square column of granite poked up through the hole. When visitors entered the room, the column was all they could see of the blade-shaped sculpture in the room below: the supreme deity, the oracle who could foretell their fates—the statue we now call the Lanzón. Like the Wizard of Oz, he was unseen, but he seemed to be all-powerful.

One archaeologist thinks that a priest leaned down toward the hole and asked questions about the future. Then, satisfied or terrified by the answers the priest relayed for the Lanzón, pilgrims exited through the same maze of halls. The ordeal was over. There was nothing they could do now but return home and wait for the oracle's predictions to come true.

If the pilgrims could have seen more than the tip of the Lanzón, they would have gasped. Made of solid stone, it weighs two tons and is almost 15 feet high. The designs carved on the huge blade-shaped rock appear to be a human figure, but jaguar fangs spring from its mouth. Its face is feline, or catlike, and the hair and eyebrows are snakes.

To us, the Lanzón looks like a big-toed cat on a bad-hair day. But the artist who carved it created an image loaded with sacred meanings. Echoing the geographical location of Chavín, the statue's raised right hand is open to the east, toward the rainforests. The lowered left hand faces back to the west, toward the coast.

The Lanzón did more than connect east and west. Its base is firmly planted in the floor. Archaeologist Richard Burger has studied the statue. He thinks that for ancient people its arms were a vertical link from the heavens above to the underworld below. East and west, up and down: Chavín, its temple, and the invisible Lanzón became the center of Andean spiritual life.

There was something else the pilgrims couldn't see: spectacular engineering that archaeologists have uncovered at Chavín. When master craftsmen built the temple, they constructed hundreds of stone-lined air ducts leading from one room to another. These provided cool, fresh air for anyone walking through the underground maze.

Archaeologists have also found drainpipes that twist through the temple and flow into canals larger than the drainpipes. One stormy day, when the skies opened and two inches of rain fell in four hours, archaeologists measured the flow of water into the temple. The measurements revealed that the pipes slowed the surge of water. Then the overflow pooled safely in underground storage chambers.

This sewer system was so complicated that Peruvian archaeologist Luis Lumbreras suspects that priests used it to convince people the **Lanzón** held supernatural powers. In 1976, Lumbreras forced 53 gallons of water into the drainpipes. Water rushed through the stone canals, over steps, and around corners.

lanzón = "lance," from Spanish. A Peruvian archaeologist gave the sculpture this name because it's shaped like a lance, or spear.

Lumbreras's fellow archaeologist Richard Burger says that the loud noise he heard that day could have frightened ancient pilgrims. More research is needed to see if this theory holds water, but scholars are certain of one thing: the religion at Chavín was so strong that it served as a connection between different Peruvian cultures. In this complicated world of mountains, coast, valleys, and rainforests, no one did everything at the same time or in the same way.

Some ancient Peruvians used llamas as pack animals; some didn't. Some made pottery, but for a long while, others wouldn't have recognized a jar if it had fallen on their heads. Some towns had sunken plazas, while others had none. In their travels, Andeans saw each other's art and technology. They united these ideas under one religion at Chavín.

The temple priests must have been lucky guys. Richard Burger thinks they were so successful at predicting the future that priests in other towns joined the party and built their own oracle centers. Who can blame them? As spokesmen for the oracles, priests could make people do exactly

CRAFTS
CREEP
ACROSS
PERU

5000 BCE
Coastal people weave
first cotton cloth

2627 BCE
People in Caral build
first sunken plazas

2000 BCE
Coastal and highland
potters make first jars

1900 BCE
Highland metalworkers
hammer sheets of gold

1840 BCE
Coastal stoneworkers
build first U-shaped
temple

400–200 BCE
Chavín cult spreads
new designs, inventions

what they told them to do. And the steady supply of free food that pilgrims brought was a nice bonus.

As the Chavín cult spread, its artistic ideas spread, too. Soon jaguar, snake, eagle, and feline designs showed up in Andean crafts, but combined in new patterns. As on the carved Lanzón, jaguar fangs snarled from human faces. Cats' paws at the end of human arms clawed the air, and writhing snakes represented human hair.

Peruvian women had been weaving images into cotton cloth since 5000 BCE. But the explosion of Chavín-style art led to new techniques. The women painted snakes with jaguar heads on fabric, and they started using llama, alpaca, and vicuña wool. The fuzzy stuff held dye much better than cotton, so the women could spin colorful wool thread and weave eagle heads into tapestries.

The weavers also discovered how to batik fabric, or coat parts of it with a waterproof substance. Waterproofing meant that dyes would color only the uncoated parts of cloth, leaving a design. They also learned to tie the cloth before dipping it in dye, a process called resist that also puts color only on certain places of the cloth. During the Chavín period, women produced tie-dyed bird designs so detailed that modern artists can't figure out how they did it.

Around 2000 BCE, Peruvian people started making simple clay pottery for cooking and storage. Thanks to Chavín influence 16 centuries later, the craft turned into an art form. Hand-shaped snakeheads decorated both sides of double-spouted jars, and painted cats with snaky tails crawled across bowls.

Metalworkers had been hammering thumb-sized sheets of gold since 1900 BCE. During the Chavín era, they had a brighter idea: to combine copper, silver, and gold. This alloy, or mixture, was stronger than pure gold, so craftsmen could solder, or melt, it onto a joint to strengthen it. The technique let them shape gold into three-dimensional figures.

From 400 to 200 BCE, the cult of Chavín cast its spell for hundreds of miles in all directions. In the highlands of Peru, archaeologists have found conch-shell trumpets like those made in Chavín. Three hundred miles south of Chavín, they've uncovered hundreds of fabric remnants woven with Chavín-style feline designs. Delicate figures made of gold have been excavated on the coast. All these wordless objects speak for the makers. They tell us that the artists were thinking about their supreme deity as they worked.

THE BIRTH OF BEDS AND BASKETS

Ancient Andean people knew how to plain-weave long before they wove images. An archaeologist has found traces of baskets and mats in Guitarrero Cave in the Andes Mountains. People lived in this cave around 8000 BCE, and historians think they must have already been skilled weavers by this time. Though they didn't weave designs, they expertly twisted, knotted, and looped plant fibers. Residents of the cave used the mats as beds and probably carried harvested crops in the baskets.

This remarkable woven wall hanging shows the supreme deity of Chavín religion, repeated many times. Chavín textiles were not the earliest in the Andean world, but Chavín craftspeople were very creative in their use of complicated weaving and dyeing techniques.

SILENCE, PLEASE

Archaeologists have found mummies from 5000 BCE in northern Chile. The discovery shows that five centuries before Egyptians preserved dead bodies, ancient Andeans invented mummification. First, the corpse was allowed to decay. Then people used ropes and canes to hold the bones in place. After stuffing the space inside the skeleton with fiber, they wrapped the body-like form in a tight cloth. Then they stitched the shape of toenails and fingernails at the ends of the mummy's hands and feet. Last, they molded a clay mask to the skull.

Like the Inca 6,500 years later, early Andean people didn't bury all of their mummies. Some stayed above ground as beloved, though mute, members of the family.

As Chavín's popularity grew, priests enlarged the temple. They erected another statue now called the Raimondi Stone, named for the Italian traveler who discovered it in 1840. Archaeologists call this god the Staff God, because he holds a staff in each hand. Sort of a Son of Lanzón, he inherited the Lanzón's fanged teeth and hair of snakes.

Carved sometime between 400 and 200 BCE, the Staff God shows Chavín art at its peak. But eventually the priests lost their power, and the cult ended. Around 200 BCE, squatters moved into the plaza, pulled stone slabs off of the circular wall, and built houses with them. The glowering stone heads were cast aside, and much of the temple crumbled. As local artists started creating their own designs, Chavín's designs went out of fashion.

Chavín wasn't the only ceremonial center in the Andean world. It wasn't the oldest or largest, either. It wasn't even original. Its temple builders borrowed the U-shape and sunken plaza designs from the coast. Sculptors and metalworkers borrowed jaguar and snake images from the rainforests. But the priests, artists, and builders of Chavín started a renaissance, or rebirth, by giving new life to old designs. Their art and inventions would influence Andean people for centuries to come. When modern Peruvians wonder how they can unite themselves as a single nation with shared beliefs, they look back 2,500 years to Chavín.

Chavín artists created remarkable works of art, such as this plaque of hammered gold. The supreme god, with his fearsome teeth and claws, reminds us of the power he held over the imaginations of ancient people.

CHAPTER 17

ON TOP OF THE WORLD
HIGHLAND EMPIRES
IN THE ANDES

Tiwanaku can be spelled at
least six different ways,
including *Tiahuanaco* and
Tihuanacu. Present-day
Bolivians who live near
the ruins of the city spell
it *Tiwanaku*.

" Pedro de Cieza de León,
The Incas, 1553 CE

Magnificent roads, fertile valleys, desolate coastal deserts—the Spanish traveler Pedro de Cieza de León thought he had seen it all. But nothing in his travels had prepared him for **Tiwanaku**. The ruins of this ancient city were sprawled below three mountains on the southeastern side of Lake Titicaca.

In 1549 CE, the 27-year-old Cieza de León described the spectacle in his journal, which was published in 1553. "Tihuanacu . . . is famous for its great buildings which, without question, are a remarkable thing to behold. Near the main dwellings is a man-made hill, built on a great stone foundation. Beyond this hill are two stone idols of human size and shape, with the features beautifully carved, so much so that they seem the work of great artists or masters. They are so large that they seem small giants."

Cieza de León asked the native people if the Inca had built the enormous structures. They laughed, because they knew the city was much, much older than the Inca Empire. The recently toppled Inca had ruled less than one century, from 1438 to 1532. In the passage of time, those decades were a mere snap of the finger.

The people of Tiwanaku first settled this high, windswept plain in 300 BCE, around the same time that the religious cult of Chavín was at its peak. Five centuries later, in 200 CE, people in Tiwanaku started a building program that carried on the ancient traditions of Chavín. It didn't matter that Tiwanaku was 600 miles away from Chavín. The idea of centering things stayed the same.

In the center of Tiwanaku, workers constructed a mound 500 feet high—a man-made mountain as sacred as the temple at Chavín. Just as at Chavín, work crews built drains and canals that led into the structure. When the level

The Kalasasaya gateway in Tiwanaku, Bolivia, was built around 600 CE. The imposing stone stairway provides an entrance to the sacred domain of the Ponce Stela in the background.

kero = "wooden drinking cup" in Quechua

of lake water was high, water flowed into the stone waterways. When water flowed out again, the mound imitated the mountain springs around Tiwanaku.

Two hundred yards away, builders dug a sunken square plaza that still stands. They surrounded the plaza with stone walls, then studded them with grimacing stone heads. In the center, builders placed the biggest of the small giants that awed Cieza de León. If the people of Tiwanaku liked centering statues, they loved making them large. The archaeologist who discovered this giant called it the Bearded Statue. Now in a museum in La Paz, Bolivia, the Bearded Statue is 23 feet tall—the largest ever found in the Andes. He holds a carved staff in one hand and a **kero** in the other.

Before the Bearded Statue was moved, he faced west, caught in a stare-down with the smaller giant. This smaller guy, called the Ponce Stela, still stands in lonely splendor.

He rises out of the center of a raised rectangular platform the size of a modern city block.

Who were these stern Goliaths? Archaeologists think back to Chavín for the answer. They see a similarity between the Staff God of Chavín and the stelae of Tiwanaku. The first holds a staff in each hand; each of the Tiwanaku gods clasps a staff to its chest.

In one corner of the raised platform, another Staff God stands guard over the top of an archway. Archaeologists call this the Gateway of the Sun, because carvings of sun rays surround the Staff God's head. He holds two staffs, and winged figures on each side are raising staffs toward him. Archaeologists think all the Staff Gods may be related to the one in Chavín. They aren't sure what the staff means, but they know that in modern Quechua-speaking communities, a staff is a sign of authority.

The Staff Gods of Tiwanaku presided over a barren setting. The high-altitude climate around Lake Titicaca is cold, and killer frosts put crops at risk several times a year. People who first settled the area in 1000 BCE needed a steady supply of food, so they invented a brilliant solution. First, they mounded earth into fields along the edge of the lake. Then they let water fill in the ditches between the raised fields. Trapped water kept the soil warm and prevented crops from freezing at night or drying out during the day.

Archaeologists have found pottery in the ditches and tested the contents with radiocarbon dating. The dates show that farmers used the raised fields for 2,000 years but stopped sometime before the Spaniards arrived. Written history agrees with this archaeological evidence, because Cieza de León didn't mention raised fields in his journal. He wrote only that people lived and planted crops on large islands in the lake.

The Ponce Stela is a dignified portrait of the Gateway God, or Staff God. The eight-foot-tall statue represents the supreme god of Tiwanaku civilization and still stands in the ruins of the city.

No one knows exactly why the fields were abandoned. But in 1981, archaeologist Clark Erikson found traces of them on the ground. He could also see them in aerial photographs. Erickson was eager to see if the ancient invention really worked. Between 1981 and 1986, he and his assistants built mounds of earth on the lake's edge and asked farmers to plant crops there. Compared to crop yield from plowed fields, the difference was astounding. Erikson proved that raised fields made early settlement around Lake Titicaca possible.

The fields were such a success that they supported an ever-growing population at Tiwanaku. At its peak, 20,000 to 34,000 ancient people lived, loved, and died there. Eventually Tiwanaku grew into a metropolis covering 30 square miles. It was the largest city in the ancient Andean world.

Around 1100 CE, drought lowered the lake level, the crops withered, and people abandoned Tiwanaku. Before disaster hit, though, the city had a huge influence on the Andean world. Archaeologists think they've found traces of this influence in Wari, 400 miles to the northeast.

Wari is a mystery to archaeologists. Was it a religious center like Chavín? A large city, a kingdom, or an empire? They can't tell. Located in a mountain valley, Wari was already a mess when Cieza de León saw it in 1549. "There are some large and very old buildings," he wrote in his journal, "which judging by the state of ruin and decay into which they have fallen, must have been there for many ages."

In the centuries after Cieza de León saw the city, farmers removed countless stones while plowing fields. They built new walls from the ancient stones. Now archaeologists don't know which walls are ancient and which are not.

Though these rocky clues are lost, archaeologists have found evidence that Wari had contact with Tiwanaku. They've excavated underground drains that channeled water through the city, just as drains in Tiwanaku's man-made mountain channeled water.

Excavations show that Wari builders constructed two- or three-story buildings divided into apartments. If the

LATER, IN MESOAMERICA

In the 15th century CE, Aztecs told a myth similar to the Inca creation myth: Two suns were born in a fire. The god of creation threw a rabbit over the face of the second sun, dimming it and turning it into the moon.

Pedro de Cieza de León, *The Incas*, 1553 CE

dwellings still stood, a modern real estate agent would have no trouble selling them. The apartments were little split-levels, with plastered floors and a step or two between each room. Each apartment included a patio with built-in benches sheltered by eaves, and a drainage hole for rainwater. The patios shared a central courtyard, where residents could meet and chat about events of the day.

Wari folks were creative decorators. They built niches into their walls for lamps, and they displayed snappy home accessories such as orange bowls and black-and-white pots. Borrowing again from Tiwanaku, the potters painted images of the Staff God on these pieces. Residents of one building might have been serious partygoers. In 1988, excavators found a room with numerous serving bowls and cups. One archaeologist thinks these are proof of feasts and drinking parties.

Drains and images of the Staff God are evidence that Tiwanaku influenced Wari, but farmers in Wari came up with an incredible idea of their own. We usually think of irrigation canals as horizontal channels from a river to a field. The Wari people built stone canals straight *up and down* steep mountain slopes.

These canals sidetracked water from mountain streams to terraced fields on the mountainside. The terraces held the water, so crops could grow even in dry years. Building the canals must have been exhausting. But after a great drought in 560 CE destroyed nearby kingdoms, the people of Wari prospered.

CLAY PEOPLE

Tiwanaku had such great influence that 1,100 years after it was abandoned, Incas claimed the world started there. In their myth, the creator god made a world of earth and sky but left it in darkness. Then he caused the sun and moon to emerge from an island in the middle of Lake Titicaca. The moon was brighter than the sun, until the jealous sun threw a handful of ashes in the moon's face and dimmed her brightness.

After the creator made the sun, moon, and constellations, he went to Tiwanaku and modeled animals and tribes of people out of clay. He painted clothes on the people and gave each tribe their food, language, and songs. Finally, he ordered them to go into caves, lakes, and hills. When he gave the word, the tribes emerged and settled in places he assigned for each one.

Craftspeople in the highland city of Wari produced a variety of beautiful decorative objects. This figurine is four inches high and was made from wood inlaid with shell, stone, and silver.

These terraced fields were used by the Inca for growing maize in high, mountain settings. By expanding the area in which maize could be grown, the Inca were able to feed vastly greater numbers of people.

CITIES COME, CITIES GO

1000 BCE
People around
Lake Titicaca invent
raised fields

300 BCE
Tiwanaku is estab-
lished on shores of
Lake Titicaca

560 CE
Wari begins a
government

700 CE
Tiwanaku becomes
largest Andean city

1000 CE
Drought destroys
Tiwanaku

1100 CE
Wari government
collapses

1440 CE
Inca claim world began
in Tiwanaku

Even with irrigated terraces, though, Wari sometimes ran out of food. No single settlement in the valley could produce enough crops to feed everyone. People had to share what they grew. If they needed more maize than they could grow, they sent colonists to raise it in other highland valleys or on the coast. In return, those places sent colonists to Wari for what they needed. This system of sharing was a bigger version of an *ayllu*, and it worked well because all the communities cooperated.

About 560 CE, Wari organized itself into a capital city with a government. Then a tricky new version of sharing developed. Haul stones for public roads, the government told the people, and grow crops in public fields. In exchange for the harvest, we'll give you free feasts. The people, who had good reason to trust the idea of sharing, fell for it.

The imitation of the old familiar give-and-take meant that the government received almost-free labor. What a deal! The plan worked so well for governments that rulers throughout the central Andes used it long after Wari was abandoned around 1100 CE.

THE MAN WITH THE GOLD EARRINGS

MOCHE ARTISTS IN COASTAL PERU

Moche comes from the word *Mochica*. This was the language that people spoke in the Moche Valley when Pedro de Cieza de León visited Cerro Blanco in the 16th century CE.

❝ Tomb of the Moche warrior-priest, Huaca Sipán, Peru, 500 CE

During the first century CE, the **Moche** people of Sipán, Peru, started work on the smallest of their three pyramids. Work crews molded mud into adobe blocks twice the size of modern bricks. The bricklayers sun-dried the blocks, set them in place, and slathered clay mortar between them. Gradually, one crew after another built a raised platform with two steps. The first stage of the smallest pyramid was complete by 100 CE.

Over the next four centuries, generations of workers added five more layers of adobe blocks to the top and sides of the original platform. Each layer was a way of asking the gods to keep drought, disease, and other bad luck away. In 500 CE, someone must have cried, "enough!" At 40 feet high, the pyramid was finally finished.

MEANWHILE, IN MESOAMERICA

The Maya king K'inich Yax K'uk' Mo' built a temple in Copán in 435 CE. Archaeologists have excavated six versions built over the original. Called the Temple of the Inscriptions, it was finally finished in 756.

huaca = "sacred" in Quechua. To the Incas, a *huaca* was any sacred object with sacred power. It could be a mountain, spring, temple, rock, or pyramid.

When building pyramids and palaces, each Moche brick maker identified his social group by pressing a particular mark into the top of his bricks. The brick makers' labor was probably a form of tax payment to the Moche rulers.

That was 1,500 years ago. Sadly, modern looters who were desperate for gold hacked a honeycomb of holes in the pyramid in just a few decades. No one knows exactly when the thefts began. But they stopped in 1986, when local police caught a gang of looters tunneling into the top with picks and shovels. As the looters dug, they stuffed sacks with gold objects, including beads that looked like owl heads.

Police showed the pieces to Walter Alva, director of a nearby museum. Like all archaeologists, Alva knew that the Moche were superb artists. The painted figures on their pottery seem almost alive, as if they might leap off the pot and land in the palm of your hand. And in the skilled hands of Moche potters, Chavín-style spouted bottles became lifelike sculptures of animals or people's heads. Moche painted pottery and sculpted vessels are so beautiful that museums all over the world collect them.

Alva also knew that in ancient times Sipán had been a backwater Moche town. It was a long 100 miles from the Moche capital city of Cerro Blanco in the Moche Valley. The **Huaca** of the Sun in Cerro Blanco was 165 feet high. It was built with 143 million bricks, each proudly signed with a maker's mark. Its sister pyramid, the Huaca of the Moon,

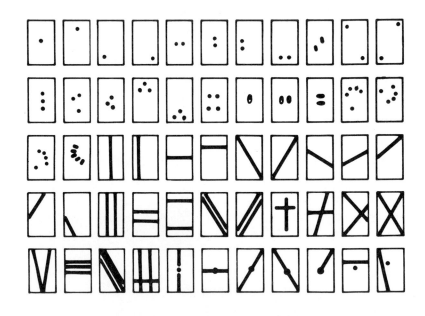

was made of 50 million bricks. Compared to these huge structures, the pyramids in Sipán were runts, especially the smallest one. Hundreds of Andean pyramids haven't been explored. Were the ones at Sipán worth the time and money? Archaeologists in the 1980s didn't think so.

And Alva knew that the Moche admired desert owls, because he had seen plenty of owl-headed priests on Moche pottery. Moche warriors identified with these fierce birds that fought only at night. But Alva had never seen anything like the owl-head beads. Only a master goldsmith could have crafted something so small and detailed. Who could have guessed the Moche were such gifted metalworkers? Maybe the pyramid held other surprises about this fascinating culture.

While police armed with submachine guns guarded the structure, Alva quickly organized a team of researchers. The team marked off an 11-foot square near the top of the pyramid. As the hot Peruvian sun broiled their heads, they burrowed down through adobe bricks until they reached a chamber.

Their first great discovery was 1,137 ceramic bowls, jars, and bottles. The bottles and jugs were shaped like

The Huaca del Sol (Pyramid of the Sun) is located in the Moche Valley, Peru. Built in the shape of a cross, the pyramid was the center of Moche government and may have been the final resting place for Moche emperors.

men—warriors with clubs or prisoners with their hands tied. This was one of the largest collections of ancient pottery ever excavated in the Americas. The diggers figured they were on to something big.

Next to the pottery, they found the bones of an ancient man. The skeleton was crumpled face forward like a rag doll, with bent knees and arms pulled toward his chest. The excavators knew that the Moche usually lay their dead on their backs when they buried them. Someone had sacrificed this poor fellow, then crammed his body into the space and filled it with pottery.

Ten feet away, the team noticed lines of gray powder seven inches wide: traces of ancient roof beams that once held up the ceiling of a room. Four inches below the gray tracks was a discovery as exciting as King Tut's tomb in Egypt or Queen Puabi's tomb in Mesopotamia.

After careful probing, the team uncovered an eight-foot by ten-foot room. In the center were traces of a wooden coffin. Remnants of red cloth lay inside the rectangular outline. These fragments were all that remained of an ancient burial shroud that once covered 461 precious objects. The stash included a solid gold headdress 23 inches across and a necklace of oversized gold and silver peanuts. The grave goods were impressive, but mere bling compared to what came next.

Slowly, the team brushed away adobe dust and uncovered the remains of a middle-aged man. Three pairs of round gold earrings lay on either side of his skull. All showed delicate craftsmanship, but one set was astonishing.

An ancient goldsmith had created a pair of three-dimensional warriors with turquoise and gold. Then he set each of the warriors into a gold disk called an ear spool. The archaeologists had to use a magnifying glass to see incredibly small knuckles on the figures' hands, and muscles on their arms and legs. Each little fighter held a removable war club and wore a removable shield. Both wore necklaces of owl-head beads, headdresses, and even little turquoise earrings. Two assistants made from confetti-sized chips of turquoise flanked each warrior.

STOP, THIEF!

When the Spaniards conquered the Inca in 1538, they heard that Moche kings were buried in the Huaca of the Sun. Believing that the pyramid held gold treasures, they changed the direction of a nearby river so that it would flow straight into the pyramid. The flood of water crumbled the adobe structure. Spaniards climbed inside, stole the gold, and melted it into bars they could carry away.

The excavators figured that the large disk earrings were miniature portraits of the buried person, so he must have been a warrior. But what had he done in life to deserve such treasures in death? And why was a sacrificed man buried in a chamber near his tomb? Then the excavators uncovered the coffins of three more men in the warrior's tomb. Oddly, one skeleton had no feet. They also found the bones of three women and the remains of a dog.

The archaeologists nicknamed their warrior the Lord of Sipán because they thought he must have been an important person. But they still knew nothing about him. They couldn't consult written history—the Moche, like other ancient Andeans, never developed a system of writing. Walter Alva turned to Christopher Donnan, co-director of the Sipán dig, for help.

Since 1974, Donnan had studied scenes the Moche painted on their pottery. He had also examined murals they painted on walls inside the Huaca of the Moon. Without written history, this artwork was as close as archaeologists could get to an eyewitness account of Moche life. After studying more than 125,000 photographs of the paintings, Donnan realized that the Moche repeated about 12 stories. As if in a play, the same actors appeared in the same scenes with the same cast of characters. Maybe one of these stories would reveal the identity of the Lord of Sipán.

Some of the painted stories were creation myths, such as the one the Inca told about the world beginning in Lake Titicaca. Donnan studied the creation paintings again. If there was a story for the Lord of Sipán, none of these paintings matched it.

Donnan examined a second theme called the Revolt of the Objects. On a painted pot showing this theme, a headdress sprouts arms and legs and chases a terrified warrior. To us, the picture seems to be a warning: keep big hats locked up! To the Moche, it was a drama showing the destruction of one group of people and the rise of another. For Donnan, the story was a dead end, because it didn't explain the identity of the Lord of Sipán, either.

This gold earring is a masterpiece of Moche craftsmanship, with lapis lazuli inlays used to highlight the figure of a great warrior. It was the prized possession of the warrior king we know as the Lord of Sipán.

FILTHY-RICH ROYALTY

King Tut of Egypt and Queen Puabi of Mesopotamia—now Iraq—weren't especially important figures in ancient history. But people remember them because, in the 1920s, archaeologists uncovered unbelievable amounts of gold ornaments in their tombs.

Then Donnan took a hard look at another subject the Moche painted on their pottery. He calls it the Sacrificial Ceremony. He had seen the ceremony many times on painted pottery and murals and thought it was a myth showing gods defeating the forces of evil. In one version, captured prisoners appear before a warrior-priest. The priest represents a god and wears a large headdress while sitting at the top of a pyramid. In another, a dog lies at the warrior-priest's feet, and assistants stand nearby. In a third painting, two women restrain a prisoner's hands while his feet are cut off.

Donnan suddenly saw a connection between these scenes and the objects found in the tomb. The Moche had actually reenacted a myth by performing sacrificial ceremonies. Then they painted their reenactment on pottery and murals. So, a similar ceremony must have actually taken place in Sipán. A real warrior-priest wearing a headdress had presided over the death of a real prisoner: the man shoved in the chamber with the pottery.

But what about the real warrior-priest's death? Another team member studied his bones and concluded that the warrior-priest was about five feet, five inches tall. He was between 35 and 45 years old—the typical life span for a Moche male. The warrior-priest's bones weren't fractured, which means he probably died a natural death some years after the sacrificial ceremony.

A scene from a Moche fine-line painted vase depicts the Sacrificial Ceremony, a religious ritual in which prisoners were sacrificed in honor of the gods. In the upper scene, a well-dressed lord, the third figure from the left, drinks from a goblet presented to him by a bird-warrior friend. In the lower scene, warriors torture and bleed captives of war.

After death, he was buried with finery that only a wealthy warrior could afford, including the large headdress and stunning earrings. Other participants in the ceremony were buried with him: two assistants, one sacrificed prisoner with missing feet, the dog, and the women. The archaeologists have no idea who these women were. Maybe they were related to the warrior-priest, or maybe they had helped with the sacrifice.

Donnan and Alva think similar rituals occurred throughout the Moche kingdom. The Moche realm was a ribbon of settlements that stretched along the coast of Peru for 350 miles. If a warrior-priest as wealthy as the Lord of Sipán lived in every Moche valley, there must have been a constant demand for master goldsmiths.

This explains why Moche artists were the finest in the Andean world—they had lots of practice. They invented molds for pottery and could produce copies of the same piece as often as they wished. They learned how to coat copper with gold, making it look like solid gold. And they turned the plain Chavín-style spouted bottles into marvelous sculptures of animals living in the kingdom, including llamas, monkeys, deer, and birds. The Moche even sculpted a pitcher with a building on top!

Moche treasures are worth money to modern looters, because some art collectors buy the objects even though such purchases are illegal. But nothing is more valuable than finding pieces in the very spot where human hands placed them so long ago. That's how we learn about ancient people, and that's the true value of the rich tombs in Sipán.

Moche potters produced thousands of lifelike portraits of people, using molds so that more than one copy of a pot could be made. Archaeologists can show that in some cases the portrait pots depict the same individual through his youth, early adulthood, and into old age.

Because of their similarity to people and their role in mythology, monkeys were a favorite subject for artisans in the Andes. This gold bead from the Moche culture shows the skill of the artist in depicting the lively, trickster personality of the spider monkey that inhabited the jungles to the east of the Andes Mountains.

CHAPTER 19

CHAN CHAN
CAPITAL CITY OF THE ANDEAN KINGDOM OF CHIMOR

"CHIMÚ MYTH

an + *onyma* = "without" + "name" in ancient Greek. An anonymous person's name is unknown.

In 1604 CE, an **anonymous** Chimú storyteller recited a long legend about his people to a Spanish historian. According to the story, the Chimú and their coastal kingdom of Chimor got off to a rocky start.

It seems that an early Chimú ruler fell under the spell of a sorceress. This beautiful woman insisted that the king change the location of the capital city. After he agreed and moved the city, his people were cursed with 30 days of floods, followed by a year of famine. As punishment, priests dragged the king to the nearby Pacific Ocean, tied his hands, and flung him in.

Revenge might be sweet, but it left the Chimú with no leader. Some time later, a speck appeared on the sea. As it came closer, the people saw that it was a boat made of light-weight balsa logs. A hero named Taycanamu was at the helm. "It is not known from whence he came," the legend says, but "he gave them to understand that a great lord . . . had sent him to govern this land. . . . The cotton cloths which he wore to cover his shameful parts are well known in these lands and the balsa of logs . . . did not come from a very distant region."

" Chimú myth, coastal Peru, 900 CE

Taycanamu led the Chimú to the Moche Valley. Then his son and grandson overpowered people in three valleys to the north and three to the south. Chimú luck had turned.

Here legend becomes real history. Around 635 CE, a rare flood destroyed Cerro Blanco, the capital city of the Moche Kingdom. When that happened, the Chimú took over all the old Moche irrigation canals and built new ones. These canals turned the scorched desert into lush fields. The Chimú built the city of **Chan Chan** in 900, and by 1465 they controlled 620 miles of farming land up and down the Peruvian coast.

chan = "sun" in Quechua

Historians who've studied the Chimú legend can't tell which kings were mythical and which were real. They're not even sure how many kings ruled Chimor. One historian thinks there might have been 10, because excavators in Chan Chan have found the ruins of 10 adobe palace compounds. Is the number an interesting coincidence? Or did each of the 10 kings build his own compound?

The answer is in the bricks. Buildings in the palace compounds were made of adobe bricks, just like the pyramids in the Moche capital of Cerro Blanco. In Cerro Blanco, each brick maker signed his handiwork with a maker's mark. But the shape of Chan Chan bricks tell a different tale. Archaeologist Alan Kolata has discovered three different shapes. Bricklayers used thin, flat bricks while building the first four compounds, thicker bricks for the next compound, and one-foot-high bricks for the last five. Kolata thinks that bricklayers built different compounds at different times—10 compounds for 10 kings.

The smallest compound spread over 17 acres, and the largest covered 51. Think of software tycoon Bill Gates, who lives on a five-acre compound with a main lodge and a separate house for servants. Or the three houses in the Kennedy family compound on Cape Cod. Or any of the eight compounds Saddam Hussein once owned in Iraq—each one has an elaborate palace, with numerous guesthouses, offices, and warehouses. Like these famous people, the leaders of Chan Chan lived in high style.

Walls around the compounds were 30 feet high and so thick that even earthquakes couldn't shake them apart. Visitors entering a compound walked through a single door in the wall. The compounds are stately and handsome, but the one very narrow door can make visitors feel almost like prisoners. This fortress-like construction would have made ancient visitors feel unsettled and would have discouraged intruders.

The single entry opened onto a spacious courtyard with benches, and a labyrinth, or maze, of passages that eventually led to another courtyard. Down the hallways were offices or living quarters for the king and his family.

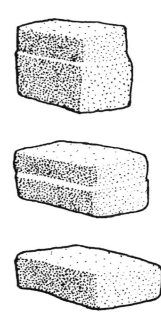

An archaeologist found three kinds of bricks in the walls of Chan Chan's many compounds. He discovered that two of the oldest, most deeply buried compounds were made with one kind of brick, and the middle compounds that were built up against the earliest ones were built with yet another kind. The uppermost, and youngest, compounds were made with yet a third type, allowing him to figure out the order in which the compounds were built based on the brick types and which walls were built up against already existing ones. Each appears to have been used for only a limited time and in sequence, so archaeologists know the order in which the compounds were built.

Nobles who served the king lived inside the compound, but in their own dwellings. These houses were within a stone's throw of the king's quarters.

Every compound had large aboveground wells about 100 feet wide and 300 feet long. Enclosed by walls, the wells tapped into underground water. They were a sign of high rank, because rain falls only once every 30 years in the parched coastal desert. A thirsty king is an unhappy king, so more than half of the wells in Chan Chan were inside royal compounds.

Beginning with the first king, people who lived in the conquered valleys had to pay tribute to Chan Chan. Llama caravans arrived regularly, delivering a steady supply of crops, metal, and woven cloth to the palace compound. The king needed somewhere to store the massive amount of goods.

Archaeologists think that builders solved the problem by constructing rows of U-shaped adobe storerooms with built-in bins. These rooms were inside the compound, and managers who staffed them were like supply sergeants in a modern army. When royal servants needed food, fabric, or jewelry for the king or his family, they simply went to a

A section of a decorated adobe wall in Chan Chan. Geometric patterns representing ocean waves, fish, and sea creatures also appear in woven textiles found in the coastal desert region.

storeroom and asked for what they wanted. Though store-room managers and palace servants lived outside the compound, they didn't have a long commute. Archaeologists have found about 3,000 dwellings just outside the walls of the second-oldest compound.

By 1450 CE, Chan Chan was the second-largest city in the Andean world, after the Inca capital of Cuzco. Proof of these high-rolling years is in the biggest compound, which measures 1/2 mile by 1/4 mile. Archaeologists call it Gran Chimú, which is Spanish for "Great Chimú." Outside the walls of Gran Chimú, they've uncovered the dwellings of 26,000 metalworkers, weavers, woodworkers, and jewelry makers.

The craftspeople lived and worked in connected houses made of cane. Rooms were small, but each house had a patio. Inside was a kitchen, where a low bench stood near the hearth, and a millstone for grinding grain sat on the floor. Imagine eating a meal with a duck nipping at your heels, or a llama snoring in the corner. Archaeologists know that animals lived in the kitchen, because they've found llama dung and bird feathers on the kitchen floors.

In other rooms, archaeologists have discovered craft items: beads, rings, and bracelets; tools for working metal; cotton for spinning; balls of wool yarn; and wood-carving tools. The many pieces of evidence suggest that these spaces were ancient workshops where artists made luxury goods for the king. The connected houses were built in tightly packed neighborhoods, with narrow alleys that led to communal wells. Living conditions weren't luxurious like those in the palace, but the rulers of Chimú knew they needed talented craftspeople. Kings allowed these artists to wear large earrings, marry among themselves, and bury their dead in private cemeteries. Still, the craftspeople had only limited privileges. Like the gated communities of today, the compound was off-limits to them.

Ten kings, ten palaces—why didn't a king move into an existing compound? Archaeologist Geoffrey Conrad thought about the question. He had read native chronicles written after the Spanish conquest. These chronicles stated

THE CARE AND FEEDING OF A KING

In 1586, a Spanish historian named Miguel Cabello listed the various duties of Chimú nobles. His descriptions give us an idea of a king's comfy lifestyle. The "Master of the Bath" made sure the king was clean. The "Royal Cook" fed him a decent breakfast. The "Purveyor of Feather-cloth Garments" dressed him in fancy clothes, and the "Steward of the Face Paint" applied streaks of color to his royal cheeks.

When a ruler went into the streets of Chan Chan, the "Blower of the Shell Trumpet" announced his coming. If a king walked, the "Preparer of the Way" went first to honor him by scattering seashell dust on the ground. When a king felt more important than usual, the "Master of the Litter and Throne" made sure that strong men carried him safely on a litter decorated with feathers and gold.

GIANT EARRINGS

An earring in the Andean world had two parts: a round tube inserted into a pierced hole in the earflap, and a disk that hung from the front of the tube. The disks were made of silver, gold, or wood. The finest ones were stamped or carved with a design.

In the Andean world, such ornaments announced a man's status level, or class, in society. Just as in Mesoamerica, only the highest nobles could wear large earrings, and Inca nobles wore the largest of all. The Spanish nickname for Inca nobles was "ore-jones" or big ears.

that before an Inca emperor died, he chose one of his sons to be the next king. But when that son took the throne, he couldn't inherit property. The chronicles also said the Inca borrowed many traditions from the Chimú. Conrad decided that the Chimú must have started the custom that the Inca later used. He calls this custom "split inheritance."

Here's how it worked: When the son of a dead Chimú king took the throne, he inherited only the title of king and the power that went with it. The rest of the family continued living in the compound and received tribute payments from land the dead king had conquered. No ruler wants to be homeless, so the first thing on the son's mind was grabbing more territory. More land meant more tribute, until he collected enough wealth to build a new palace

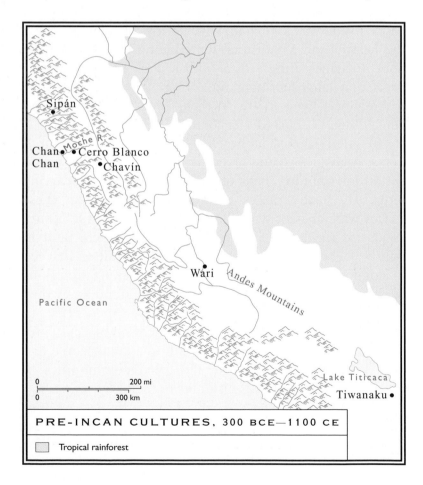

PRE-INCAN CULTURES, 300 BCE—1100 CE

Tropical rainforest

compound. The palace became the new king's home in both life and in death.

When a ruler of Chimor died, his body was mummified and buried within the compound. Then bricklayers built a low platform over the grave. Archaeologists have found from 15 to 100 shafts built into each of Chan Chan's burial platforms. About eight feet deep, these storage holes were like closets that opened from the top. Looters have robbed most of them, but luckily, they missed a few. Excavators found a shaft that was four feet wide and five feet long. Inside, they discovered the remains of fine pottery, looms, fabric, and gold artwork. The objects help archaeologists understand the purpose of the shafts.

The expression "You can't take it with you" means that people can't take belongings with them when they die. This would have sounded like nonsense to people in the ancient Andean world. They believed that a dead body went to another world, so naturally the body would need a drinking cup, clothes, and jewelry. Ordinary people were buried with just a few items. Important officials like the warrior-priest of Sipán went to the afterlife with enough goods to start a fancy jewelry store. Chimú kings got the best deal of all, because their families kept them well supplied for eternity.

Just as you wouldn't go through life wearing the same clothes or drinking from the same glass, a dead Chimú king needed new items every now and then. His family took care of his tomb, passing the responsibility on to their children, and so on, down through the generations. Each set of descendants built additions to the platform tomb and filled the shafts with a fresh supply of goods. The descendants never ran out of luxury items, because they had inherited their ancestors' wealth.

The split inheritance system worked well for hundreds of years. But as one ruler followed another, they had to go farther away from Chan Chan and add new valleys to the kingdom. Chimú may have become too large to control—the last few compounds built in Chan Chan were smaller, with fewer storerooms.

As tribute dried up, Chimú kings lost their status. A

THE RISE AND FALL OF CHIMÚ

635 CE
Chimú take over Moche irrigation canals

900 CE
Chimú build Chan Chan, expand canals

1465 CE
Chimú control 620 miles of farmland

1465 CE
Inca cut off water supply to Chan Chan

1470 CE
Inca defeat Chimú

1604 CE
Chimú descendant recounts legend to historian

Chimú artisans and architects figured out clever ways to use adobe bricks to form geometric decorations for their buildings, as can be appreciated in this view of the Tschudi Compound.

weak king means a weak army, because no one follows orders. When the Inca arrived in Chan Chan in 1465, the last Chimú ruler was unable to defeat their forces. With no warriors to stop them, the Inca changed the course of the rivers and cut off the city's water supply. The Chimú had two choices: they could die of thirst or surrender. In 1470, they chose defeat, and the Inca absorbed the great kingdom of Chimor into their mighty empire.

CHAPTER 20

CUZCO RULES
THE INCA IN THE LAND OF THE FOUR QUARTERS

❝ BERNABÉ COBO

Pachacuti never expected to be an emperor. Why would he? His father ruled Cuzco, a small Inca town in the Andes Mountains. But it was an insignificant place—a tiny mole, a fleck of dust on the face of the vast Andean world. And the Inca were only one of many groups of people who lived in this world. They were no smarter than the Chanca to the north, and certainly not as powerful as the Chimú on the coast.

Besides, **Pachacuti**'s father had already chosen another son as his successor. All of that changed in 1438 CE, when the Chanca people threatened to attack Cuzco. Afraid of defeat by the more powerful Chanca army, the Inca ruler and his favored son slunk away to the safety of a mountain fort. Pachacuti might have been the unfavored son, but he was no coward. He took command of Inca generals and warriors in Cuzco. When the Chanca roared into the village, the Inca stood their ground with slingshots and clubs.

In 1569, Inca historians told a story about this battle to a Spanish writer. At a key moment in combat, Pachacuti cried out that the very stones in the field were turning into men to help him. Apparently, the Inca were such brave fighters that every man had the strength of many. When the Inca won, Pachacuti was so grateful that he gathered all the stones from the battleground. Believing that the rocks were now *huacas*, or sacred objects, he placed them in religious shrines in Cuzco. Then he proceeded to crown himself king of the Inca.

{ *pachacuti* = "cataclysm," or "He Who Remakes the World" in Quecha. Cataclysm comes from the ancient Greek word "cataclysmos," which means deluge, or flood.

The great Inca ruler Pachacuti holds a wooden shield and a sling for hurling rocks.

HOW TO
TIE UP THE SUN

Between 1460 and 1470, Pachacuti built Machu Picchu, which means "manly peak." This magnificent city is 8,000 feet high in the Andes Mountains and has 200 buildings. Most of them were dwellings for 1,200 women, children, and priests. To construct the buildings, Inca stonemasons cut and polished huge granite rocks. The craftsmen fitted the stones together so tightly that it's impossible to insert a knife blade between them.

Historians don't think that Machu Picchu was a fortress or center of trade. Instead, Pachacuti must have wanted a religious retreat, because a ceremonial column of stone stands in the city. The Inca called these stones *intihuatana*, or "for tying of the sun" in Quechua. In early winter, as the days grew shorter, a priest held a ceremony at the column. He "tied" the sun to the stone to keep daylight from disappearing forever.

topa inca = "royal inca" in Quechua }

The mountaintop retreat of Machu Picchu, south of Cuzco, is the best-preserved Inca site in the Andes. It escaped the attention of the Spaniards and their descendants until local guides led the American archaeologist Hiram Bingham there in 1911.

Pachacuti never met Itzcoatl, whose victory over a rival city in the same year started the Aztec Empire in Mesoamerica, far to the north. But the two rulers had a lot in common.

Itzcoatl rewrote history to suit himself, and Pachacuti changed history, too. He commanded that the Inca erase his brother's name from memory, though he did allow them to remember his disgraced father. In Mexico, Itzcoatl turned Tenochtitlan into a city that seemed to float on water. In Peru, Pachacuti rebuilt Cuzco as a showcase with paved streets, palaces, and temples sheathed in gold.

Victory was as addictive for Pachacuti as it was for Itzcoatl. Over the next 97 years, he and his son, **Topa Inca**, and *his* son, Huayna Capac, toppled other kingdoms in the Andean world, including the Chimú Empire. From southern Ecuador to northern Chile and every kingdom in between—40,000 Inca controlled 10 million non-Inca subjects.

Pachacuti reshaped the kingdoms as if they were fresh clay. His first step was forcing everyone to learn Quechua, the language the Inca spoke and that many Peruvians still speak today. Next, he claimed that his ancestors had been born in Lake Titicaca—the birthplace of Inti, god of the sun. The coincidence was rigged, of course, but it worked. Pachacuti turned himself into the son of a god.

Pachacuti didn't stop there. Bernabé Cobo, a Spanish priest, lived in Cuzco in the early 1600s. In 1653, he wrote a history of the Inca and retold a story that Pachacuti invented to back up his claim of royal descent. The emperor said that as a young man, he looked into a crystal tablet and saw Inti. "Come here, my child," Inti told Pachacuti in the invented story. "Have no fear, for I am your father the Sun; I know that you will subjugate [conquer] many nations and take care to honor me and remember me in your sacrifices."

What's more, Pachacuti claimed that the Staff God of ancient Chavín and Tiwanaku was none other than Inti. By moving the gods around in people's minds, he made himself part of a divine family. It was the oldest royal trick in the world: claim that you're a god, and people will follow orders.

As the empire grew, Pachacuti split it into four sections: the Land of Four Quarters, or Tawantinsuyu in the Quechua language. Then he divided each quarter into 20 smaller districts—80 in all. Even the great Pachacuti couldn't be in 80 places at once. Sometimes he sent Inca commanders to these districts so they could keep tabs on taxes the population owed him. More often, he appointed a local ruler as commander. Conquered people preferred this method. After all, who wants a nosy outsider from Cuzco taking charge?

There was a catch to the system, though. Sons of local rulers lived as hostages in Cuzco, where they attended school. For four years, Inca teachers taught them how to

> Bernabé Cobo, *History of the Inca Empire*, 1653

MAJOR GODS OF THE ANDES

REALM	INCA NAME	ENGLISH TRANSLATION
creation	Viracocha	*Ancient foundation, Lord, Instructor of the World*
sun	Inti	*Sun*
thunder	Ilayapa	*Thunder, Lightning*
moon	Mama-kilyq	*Mother Moon*

SORE FEET

Teachers in the Cuzco schools were strict, but not as strict as they wanted to be. According to the rules, they could beat a student only once a day. And they could give only 10 blows to the soles of the boy's feet—not one lick more!

Inca stonemasons used massive stone blocks to build the great fortress of Sacsahuaman above the city of Cuzco. The rocks are so tightly fitted together that a knife blade cannot be slipped between the joints.

speak Quechua and made them memorize Pachacuti's new version of Inca religion. If daddy cheated Pachacuti out of his taxes, the emperor punished or killed his son. No wonder local rulers kept excellent tax records! And they had lots of records to keep, because Pachacuti further divided the land within each district.

He gave local people some fields for their own crops and set aside other fields for religious shrines. The rest belonged to him. Pachacuti taxed almost everyone, but they couldn't pay with money because Peru had no currency. So people paid him with beads of sweat. Using the system that began in Wari, the emperor forced them to farm his fields, then turn over the harvest to the local commander.

There were plenty of royal fields to farm, because Pachacuti borrowed farming techniques that Wari people had developed centuries before. Their stone irrigation canals ran from high mountain springs down into terraced slopes. Build more canals and fields throughout the empire, Pachacuti ordered, and put them on the highest mountains! So the people whom Pachacuti conquered turned even the steepest slopes into stepped fields for growing maize.

More maize meant more grain to make a thick beer called *chicha*. This mild brew was the favorite alcoholic beverage of the Andean world. It came in handy for the next part of Pachacuti's plan.

Using the old Wari system of "give to me, I'll give to you," army commanders arranged free feasts in exchange for the tax-labor. A typical party featured flute and drum music, dancing, and lots of food and *chicha*. Sometimes commanders ran out of things for local people to do. Pachacuti's son, Topa Inca, once insisted that workers move an entire hill from one place to another just so they would earn their feast.

The United States has an Internal Revenue Service that makes sure people pay taxes. Inca commanders had their own kind of IRS—we could call it the Inca Revenue Service—staffed with local men. Whereas Mesoamericans counted by 20—10 fingers and 10 toes—the Inca used the decimal system and counted by 10. The taxmen carefully recorded population, lengths of cloth, and harvested crops in decimal numbers. They even knew exactly how many llamas people owned.

To keep track of the numbers, the men used a counting device called a *khipu*, or "knot" in Quechua. Archaeologists have uncovered *khipus* in the dry coastal valleys of Peru. These date back to 750 CE, which shows that Pachacuti made use of another old idea. A *khipu* was a group of strings hanging from a main horizontal cord. Substrings of various colors dangled from the vertical strings. The Inca tied knots at various places on all of the strings.

Archaeologists still don't know what the different colors of the strings meant. But in 1926, a historian figured out that the Inca used three different kinds of knots: one kind stood for the number one, another for the numbers two through nine, and another for all decimal values above nine: 10, 100, 1,000, and so forth. Zeros were simply an unknotted place on the string.

The emperor always knew the number of people and amount of extra goods in his empire, because messengers brought *khipus* to him in Cuzco. There, an expert called a *Khiupukamayoq* interpreted the knots for him.

Messengers also relayed goods to warehouses by running up, down, and across the ladder of roads that Pedro de Cieza de León saw in 1548. The messenger picked up a package, ran to the next storehouse on the royal road, and relayed it to another messenger. Packages traveled an average of 150 miles in one day. Though Cuzco was in the mountains, the emperor could eat fresh anchovies from the

Inca officials recorded information with a khipu, *or knotted string device. By tying knots of different sizes in certain places along the strings, they could keep track of taxpayers and goods and save stories about Inca history and religion.*

CHEW, SPIT, WAIT, DRINK

Ancient Andean people drank *chicha* as if it were water. They served it at every meal, though they were careful not to become drunk. Intoxication was allowed only at religious festivals, where it was part of sacred ceremonies. To make *chicha*, Inca women chewed raw corn and spat the mashed pulp into pottery jars. Then the liquid fermented until it was part alcohol. The longer the *chicha* sat, the more alcohol it would contain. People in parts of South America still make *chicha*. In Bolivia, they use ground peanuts instead of corn. In the Amazon rainforests, women mash manioc roots.

MUMMIES ON THE MOVE

As in Chimú, a royal Inca family became guardians of their dead king and made sure he enjoyed an active social life. Sometimes they took him to visit another mummy, or a different royal family brought their mummy to visit him.

When people in Cuzco held a celebration, family servants carried the royal mummy bundle to the main square and sat him in a row with other royal mummies. Then the servants lit a fire and burned food in front of the mummies so their souls could eat. To help wash down the food, servants filled gold pitchers with *chicha* and toasted each other in the name of their particular mummy.

coast, because runners delivered them in just two days. Not bad for a human delivery truck!

Warehouses were key to the success of this Inca version of the Pony Express. Local laborers improved the ancient warehouses that *ayllus* had built thousands of years earlier. They added two sets of storehouses in each district: one for crops from the emperor's fields, the other for surplus goods from people's fields. All cities in the empire had storehouses, too, with the largest number in Cuzco.

These structures held extra food, clothing, and weapons for warriors who policed the empire. But the emperors also saved food for the people. If crops failed in one part of the empire, rulers sent relief supplies from the storehouses. Few people went hungry in the Inca Empire.

Still, the emperors had more fine cloth, food, pottery, and jewelry than they could ever use. Why did they keep expanding the empire?

Borrowing again from an older culture, Pachacuti adopted the Chimú idea of split inheritance. Just as in the kingdom of Chimor, the surviving royal family and their descendants used that wealth to maintain the palace as a shrine to the mummified dead king.

Mummies and split inheritance—terraced slopes—working for feasts—*khipus*—warehouses—old gods with new names—these customs show that the Inca were great imitators of older cultures. But Pachacuti made sure that the Inca got all the credit. He proclaimed that people who had lived before the Inca were uncivilized savages. His official Inca history fooled everyone, including Spanish historians, for a long while.

Pachacuti was clever, but he couldn't trick time. He died in 1471. Four hundred years later, archaeologists started excavating ancient cities in the Andean world. Now they've traced the traditions of the Inca Empire back to earlier cultures in Chavín, Tiwanaku, Wari, and Chimú. Though Pachacuti tried to erase thousands of years of pre-Inca history, he didn't succeed. As it turns out, Inca inventions weren't Inca, after all.

CHAPTER 21

CHOSEN GIRLS AND BREECHCLOTH BOYS
LIFE IN THE INCA EMPIRE

Pachacuti, Topa Inca, and his son Huayna Capac were more than just a dynasty of emperors. In less than 60 years, they created the largest Bronze Age, or bronze tool making, civilization in the world. But they succeeded only because they had almost total control of Inca subjects, including children. For special occasions such as a festival, Inca priests traveled through the empire. They chose one perfect child under the age of ten as a sacrifice to the gods. Luckily, priests passed over those with the slightest spot or blemish, so all but one child lived.

An Inca child's life started peacefully enough. A baby spent the first four days of life sheltered in its mother's arms. Then it slept in a snug cradle made of boards and cushioned with a folded shawl. When a mother wanted to go somewhere, she tied the cradle to her back with another shawl.

Around the time that children learned to walk, they received their childhood names in a hair-cutting ceremony. Friends and relatives gathered for a feast with drinking and dancing. Then the oldest uncle cut the child's hair and nails and assigned a temporary name.

Even small children were disciplined and had to help with

An Inca clay watering vessel. Made in the shape of a traditional Andean foot plow, it features an ear of corn and a storage vessel for maize on top, and so depicts all stages of the planting and harvesting of the crop.

HARD ROCK, HEAVY METAL

In the 1820s, a Danish archaeologist came up with a three-age system to classify human tool-making progress. Stone Age people made both crude and sophisticated tools from stone. They entered the Bronze Age when they discovered how to make bronze tools from an alloy, or mix, of copper and tin.

Iron isn't as heavy as bronze, but it's harder and occurs naturally mixed in with rock. People entered the Iron Age when they learned how to melt the iron out of rock. Then blacksmiths made tools such as knives by heating, pounding, and cooling the iron. No ancient American culture ever entered the Iron Age, and Mesoamericans never reached the Bronze Age.

THE CIRCLE OF LIFE

It's hard to understand human sacrifice. But if we look at it through Inca eyes, they actually placed a high value on human life. By choosing only one child—the most perfect one—they made it possible for all other little ones to live. And that one child kept the circle of life going. The Inca planted a seed, watched it grow into a plant when the gods sent sunshine and rain, harvested the fruit of the plant, and ate it so they could stay alive. Then they thanked the gods with the most precious thing they could give back to them—a perfect child—and the circle began again. In the Inca world, it was a high honor to be chosen for sacrifice.

chores. Sometimes boys hunted birds for food. Or a boy's mother might ask him to carry a baby sibling in a blanket on his back. Girls ground maize, spun thread, and hauled wood for the family hearth. As they grew older, both boys and girls worked in the fields and herded llamas.

Like children everywhere, of course, Inca boys and girls managed to find some fun. Girls spun tops through the air, while boys ran foot races and held slingshot contests. In 1653, Spanish historian Bernabé Cobo wrote down the names of Inca games, though not the rules. Young people played "mountain lion," "one pile after another," and a ball game called "potato chief."

Life turned serious for girls at the age of ten. A royal official visited every village in the empire, scouting for beautiful, well-mannered girls. He chose some for sacrifice to the sun god, Inti. But first, he assured parents that their daughters would live through eternity in peace and contentment.

The rest of the girls traveled to a "House of the Chosen Women," where they spent the remainder of their childhoods. Over the next four years, they learned the arts of cooking, brewing *chicha*, spinning thread, weaving, and sewing. In 1567, Inca historian Guamán Poma drew a picture of chosen girls. It's easy to see that at least one girl—the one behind the hand spindle—isn't happy with her lot in life.

The Inca built a "House of the Chosen Women" in each quarter of the empire. While excavating an Inca city in the 1980s, archaeologists uncovered 50 buildings sur-

"Disobedience was punished even in the nursery by pinching the children's ears. As old people grew their fingernails long, the little ears were often pierced through from side to side."

Guamán Poma, *Letters to a King*, 1567 CE

SETIMO CALLE
TOCI LAGOCVAMRA

OTABO CALLE
PVCIIACOC

An Inca boy (left) hunts birds by slinging a rock in this drawing by Guamán Poma. An Inca girl (right) spins a top.

rounded by a wall. They think this compound was built for Chosen Women.

If so, the girls and women were well protected from intruders. Approved visitors entered through a single doorway in the wall. They passed through a small courtyard and a tiny square building, then entered a large inner courtyard. Dormitory-like buildings for living quarters and workshops surrounded the courtyard. Inside the workshops, the archaeologists found weaving tools made of bone, dozens of hand spindles for spinning thread, and thousands of large jars for brewing *chicha*—all tools that Chosen Women would have used.

Four years of work and supervision, away from their families—it's no wonder one of the girls in Guamán Poma's picture seems miserable. After the girls reached puberty, the priests classified them again. Any girl who wasn't sacrificed became a **Mama Kona**.

Some Mama Konas remained in the compound and taught the young girls. Others were assigned to distant towns, where they cared for shrines and prepared special dishes and *chicha* for festivals. A Mama Kona could never

{ *mama kona* = "mother" + "chosen woman" in Quechua

❝ Guamán Poma, *Letters to a King*, 1567 CE

A Chosen Woman instructs Chosen Girls. Particularly beautiful and talented girls were taken to live in special compounds and taught to weave fine cloth and brew beer.

❝ Bernabé Cobo, *Inca Religion and Customs*, 1653 CE

have a boyfriend or marry. If a priest caught her talking to a man, he hanged her by her hair until death. "In their whole life," Guamán Poma wrote in 1567, "they were never allowed to speak to a man."

And what happened to girls who weren't chosen? Guamán Poma wrote that the Inca called them the "left-out" ones. When puberty arrived, a girl's parents kept her in the house, where she fasted for two days without any food. On the third day, the mother gave her a ration of raw maize and commanded her not to die of hunger.

On the fourth day, the mother bathed her daughter, combed and braided her hair, then dressed her in new clothes and stylish white wool sandals. A two-day family feast followed, probably to the great relief of the famished daughter. When the feast was over, the oldest uncle gave her a grown-up name. Common Quechua names for women meant egg, pure, star, or gold.

The maturity celebration for boys was a public affair. Every December, all 14-year-old boys in a village or town gathered for a festival. Each was given a breechcloth—a long six-inch-wide strip of cloth that the boy passed between his legs, then up and under a narrow belt around his waist. He flipped the extra cloth over the belt so that it hung down to the front and back of his thighs. Then an uncle gave him a manly new name, such as jaguar, dragon, tobacco, or hawk.

Every Inca man and woman—except Chosen Women—was expected to marry. Bernabé Cobo wrote in 1653 that the "boys were from 15 to 20 years old, and the girls were a little younger." Young people could choose their mates, but they weren't officially engaged until the commander of the district approved. When he visited a village, he placed the young men in a line facing the young women. Each man pointed to his future bride. Then she stood behind him. If two men wanted the same woman, the commander made the decision in the name of the emperor. The long arm of royal rule controlled even marriage, but at least emperors had no say in wedding ceremonies. These customs varied according to district.

The Inca "chosen women" were separated from the rest of the community at an early age in order to serve the emperor by creating magnificent cloth, textiles, and beer. The fine cloth used in this figurine representing a chosen woman was quite simple compared with the elaborate textiles they produced, which were given away by the Inca emperor to reward his most valued subjects.

In a typical noble wedding, the groom and his family visited the bride's home. He placed a sandal on her right foot, Cinderella-style. Then they all walked to the groom's house, where she gave him clothes and a gold or silver ornament. Both sets of parents presented gifts and offered advice on marriage. The wedding ended with a feast, just as many weddings today end with a reception.

Marriage usually meant children. The birth of a baby in a farming family was a joyful occasion, because the district commander assigned new fields every year. The larger the family, the more land it could farm for its own needs. Parents could also trade their children's labor. If one family needed help in the fields, a neighbor's children lent a hand and vice versa.

But Inca emperors interrupted this spirit of cooperation when they moved rebellious people to other parts of the empire. Any of the strict rules could set off a revolt. People in a coastal town might decide their grown children didn't need royal approval for engagements. Some people refused to speak Quechua, the official language of the empire. And some newly conquered people weren't ready to give in without a fight.

To put down such mutinies, Inca emperors might move members of a rebellious tribe to another district. Then they replaced them with people from somewhere else who were familiar with Inca customs and Quechua. Or the emperor left rebels in place but imported people who made sure they joined Team Inca. Both the exiles and the incoming groups were called *mitmaq* (Quechua for "displaced people").

FROM HEAD TO TOE

No Inca women pierced their ears, but some noble women wore beaded necklaces made from seashells or bones. All women wore ankle-length dresses tied at the waist with a sash. Over the dress, they wore a cape fastened at the chest with a gold, silver, or copper pin. Sandals for both men and women were made from the hide of a llama's neck. Only noble men and women could decorate their sandal straps with gold ornaments.

A noble bride usually gave her husband a headband and a fine wool tunic. Every Inca man wore a knee-length sleeveless sack over his breechcloth and a large cloak around his shoulders. But only a nobleman's tunic was woven all over with colorful geometric designs inside small squares.

THE RISE
AND FALL
OF THE INCA
EMPIRE

1438 CE
Pachacuti becomes
emperor

1471 CE
Pachacuti's son, Topa
Inca, becomes emperor

1493 CE
Huayna Capac, Topa
Inca's son, becomes
emperor

1527 CE
Huayna Capac dies

1532 CE
Franciso Pizarro
executes Atahualpa,
Huayna Capac's son

In 1493, Huayna Capac inherited the throne. At that point, the empire was about 55 years old. In age, it was an infant compared to previous Andean empires, and the baby had growing pains. Revolts were a constant problem. Conquered people in some districts were so defiant that *mitmaq* outnumbered original residents.

Even worse, Huayna Capac was running out of land that would bring more tribute. He spent years fighting for a scrap of new territory in northern Ecuador so he could build the palace that would one day hold his mummified body. He was even considering building a second capital city in Ecuador. This idea didn't sit well with Inca nobles in Cuzco. Trouble was already brewing for Huayna Capac when an unexpected disaster occurred.

In keeping with Pachacuti's tradition of telling tales, the Inca told a story about Huayna Capac's last days: One night he and his army were camped on the coast of Ecuador. The emperor had a vision—500,000 ghosts were gathered around the camp, ready to attack. Alarmed, he returned to Quito.

Soon a runner wearing a black cloak arrived, carrying a small box. Huayna Capac told him to open it, but the messenger refused. The god of creation, he said, had sent him with strict orders. Only the emperor should open the mysterious container. When Huayna Capac unfastened the cover, moths and butterflies swarmed out. These winged creatures were the pestilence, or epidemic, that killed all of Huayna Capac's army and then the emperor himself.

The last part of the myth is true; the pestilence was the smallpox virus. Huanya Capac, the emperor who stood so proudly in his litter in 1493, died from the disease in 1527. Just as Hernán Cortés had luck on his side when he conquered the Aztec Empire, the Spanish conquistador Francisco Pizarro was a very fortunate man. With no emperor, the empire was too divided to stop his conquest in 1532.

Some scholars think that revolts and the endless quest for land would have wrecked the empire, anyway. But we'll never know, because the Spaniards supplied a different—and tragic—conclusion to the story of the Inca Empire.

EPILOGUE
THE LEGACY OF
THE ANCIENT AMERICAS

It might seem that Mesoamerica and the Andean world have nothing to do with you. But your stomach would tell you otherwise. Mesoamericans began planting wild maize in 5000 BCE. Both livestock and people all over the world still eat it—including you, if you've ever munched popcorn or enjoyed corn-on-the-cob.

Imagine a pizza without tomatoes. Until the Spanish conquest, Europeans had never laid eyes on this juicy fruit. What would Halloween be without pumpkins, which were first grown in Mesoamerica? Or Thanksgiving without turkeys?

Thousands of years ago, Andean people started planting wild potatoes. If it weren't for these ancient farmers, you might never have eaten baked potatoes or french fries. The Andean people also developed the peanuts that get mashed into peanut butter you eat with jelly. Oddly, the one plant with no food value traveled the fastest from the Americas to the rest of the world. In less than a year after the Spanish conquest, people around the globe were smoking tobacco.

Of course, gold and silver in the Americas were more valuable to the Spaniards than food and tobacco. These precious metals made a difference in the world's economy, including that of Spain. The vast amounts of gold and silver were exciting at first, and they made some explorers rich. But over the long haul, land and labor stolen from native-born Americans created more wealth for Europeans than bars of silver and gold.

The great encounter also led to changes in the Americas. Beasts of burden, chickens, cattle, sheep, goats—all of these animals benefited native-born people. European technology helped people, too—a metal plow pulled by oxen was a great improvement over the digging sticks that farmers used before the Spaniards arrived. Other technologies reached the Americas, too: mills for grinding, wheeled carts and carriages, and nautical, or sea-going, engineering. But these technologies helped the Spanish newcomers more than they helped the native people.

The sad truth is that most peoples in the Americas suffered great losses after the Spaniards arrived. Cortés himself lamented that he felt he had to destroy Tenochtitlan in order to capture it. And many of the native people who managed to survive infectious diseases were worked to death in gold and silver mines. In 1492, Christopher Columbus made his first fateful voyage to the Americas. Within a century of his arrival, the population in the Americas was one-tenth of what it had been.

The loss of culture was as heartbreaking as the loss of human life. When a Spanish priest destroyed thousands of Mayan books, he said, "They contained nothing but superstitions and lies of the devil, so we burned them all, which caused them [the people] great affliction." But if the Spaniards had chosen to read the books, they could have learned a great deal about astronomy and solar and lunar cycles. If the Spaniards had just listened, the native people would have taught them new ways of farming.

But all was not—and is not—lost. Native and colonial chronicles help us understand how native people lived, worked, played, and learned. Archaeology is an even better source of information. Archaeological remains let us picture the lives of ordinary people, not just priests and rulers who appear in hieroglyphic books, pottery portraits, and stone monuments. Things left behind in houses, streets and waterworks, temples and royal palaces, are a true record of how people lived.

People in Mesoamerica and the Andean world today are thrilled when they discover the amazing accomplishments of their ancestors. They're keenly interested in sharing this history with others. If you visit the Americas, you'll find that the descendants of the Mexica, Maya, and Inca have much to be proud of: vibrant cultures, beautiful arts and crafts, and a deep appreciation of their enchanted lands.

TIMELINE

The centuries BCE and CE are mirror images of each other. The years go backwards before the Year 1 CE. So someone born in 2000 BCE who died in 1935 BCE would have lived to be 65 years old. On both sides of the "mirror," the 200s can also be called the 3rd century, the 900s are called the 10th century and so on—BCE as well as CE.

5000 BCE
Maize agriculture begins in Mesoamerica

5000–3700 BCE
Andean people begin to grow cotton and weave cloth

3000 BCE
Villages established at Aspero and Caral

2700 BCE
Construction begins on Pirámide Mayor at Caral

2000 BCE
First villages appear in Mesoamerica

1900 BCE
Highland Peruvians hammer sheets of gold

1800 BCE
Pottery making begins in Peru

1300 BCE
Village life is well established in Mesoamerica

1150 BCE
Olmec town of San Lorenzo rises

900 BCE
Tierras Largas house in Oaxaca abandoned; Olmec settlement of San Lorenzo abandoned; Olmec establish La Venta

600 BCE
Chavín de Huántar first settled

500 BCE
One Earthquake sacrificed at San José Mogote; Zapotec capital of Monte Albán founded

400 BCE
Chavín de Huántar becomes important religious and trade center

350 BCE
El Mirador, first Maya city, rises

300 BCE
Tiwanaku first settled

250 BCE
El Mirador flourishes

200 BCE
Monte Albán becomes powerful city

1 CE
City of Teotihuacan founded

100 CE
Moche people begin building Huacas of the Sun and Moon

200 CE
Tiwanaku residents begin massive building effort

400 CE
125,000 people live in Teotihuacan

426 CE
K'inich Yax K'uk' Mo' travels from Teotihuacan to Copán

550 CE
Temples burned in Teotihuacan

600 CE
Wari becomes powerful city

612 CE
Lady Sak K'uk' becomes Queen of Palenque

615 CE
Pakal becomes King of Palenque

763 CE
Altar Q is dedicated by Copán's last ruler

800 CE
Aguateca invaded; Putún Maya seafaring merchants gain power; Wari's influence and power end

900 CE
Monte Albán population shrinks to only a few thousand; Tula Chico is burned; Tula Grande is built; Chimú found city of Chan Chan

950 CE
Tula Grande becomes second-largest city in Central Mexico

1000 CE
Tiwanaku abandoned

1438 CE
Itzcoatl establishes Aztec Triple Alliance; Pachacuti defeats the Chanca; Inca expansion begins

1470 CE
Inca Empire conquers Chimú Empire

1493 CE
Huayna Capac becomes Inca Emperor

1502 CE
Columbus encounters Maya canoe

1519 CE
Cortés arrives on the shores of Mexico

1521 CE
Cortés and native allies conquer Aztec Triple Alliance

1525 CE
Huayna Capac dies; his sons struggle for power

1526 CE
Smallpox invades South America

1532 CE
Francisco Pizarro conquers Inca Empire

1535 CE
Pedro de Cieza de León arrives in Peru; Guamán Poma is born in Peru

1567 CE
Guamán Poma begins a letter to the king of Spain

FURTHER READING

Entries with 🔲 *indicate primary source material.*

GENERAL WORKS ON THE ANCIENT AMERICAS

Cobb, Vicki. *This Place Is High: The Andes Mountains of South America.* New York: Walker Books, 1993.

🔲 Coe, Michael D., and Rex Koontz. *Mexico: From the Olmecs to the Aztecs.* 5th ed., rev. and expanded. London: Thames and Hudson, 2002.

🔲 Coe, Sophie, and Michael Coe. *The True History of Chocolate.* London: Thames and Hudson, 1996.

Fritz, Jean. *Around the World in a Hundred Years: From Henry the Navigator to Magellan.* New York: Putnam, 1998.

Laughton, Timothy. *The Maya: Life, Myth, and Art.* New York: Abrams, 1998.

Lepore, Jill. *Encounters in the New World: A History in Documents.* New York: Oxford University Press, 2002.

Lourie, Peter. *Lost Treasure of the Inca.* Honesdale, Pa.: Boyds Mills Press, 1999.

MacDonald, Fiona. *How Would You Survive as an Aztec?* New York: Franklin Watts, 1997.

Marrin, Albert. *Aztecs and Spaniards.* New York: Atheneum, 1986.

Marrin, Albert. *Inca and Spaniard (Pizarro and the Conquest of Peru). Book Two: The Gold of Cuzco.* New York: Atheneum, 1989

Meyer, Carolyn. *The Mystery of the Ancient Maya.* New York: Atheneum, 1995.

Pohl, John M. D. *Exploring Mesoamerica.* New York: Oxford University Press, 1999.

Steele, Philip. *The Aztec News.* New York: Candlewick Press, 2000.

Von Hagen, Adriana, and Craig Morris. *The Cities of the Ancient Andes.* New York: Thames and Hudson, 1998.

Wood, Tim. *The Aztecs.* New York: Viking, 1992.

Wood, Tim. *The Incas.* New York: Viking, 1996.

DICTIONARIES AND ENCYCLOPEDIAS

Carrasco, Davíd, ed. *The Oxford Encyclopedia of Mesoamerican Cultures: The Civilizations of Mexico and Central America.* New York: Oxford University Press, 2001.

Evans, Susan Toby, and David L. Webster, eds. *Archaeology of Ancient Mexico and Central America: An Encyclopedia.* New York: Garland, 2001.

BIOGRAPHY

Calvert, Patricia. *Hernando Cortes: Fortune Favored the Bold.* New York: Benchmark, 2002.

Meltzer, Milton. *Francisco Pizarro: The Conquest of Peru.* New York: Benchmark, 2004.

ART

Donnan, Christopher B. *Moche Portraits from Ancient Peru.* Austin: University of Texas Press, 2004.

Miller, Mary. *Maya Art and Architecture.* London: Thames and Hudson, 1999.

Pasztory, Esther. *Aztec Art.* New York: Abrams, 1983.

Stone-Miller, Rebecca. *Art of the Andes: From Chavín to Inca.* 2nd ed. London: Thames and Hudson, 2002.

NATIVE CHRONICLES

Huamán Poma (Don Felipe Huamán Poma de Ayala), *Letter to a King: A Picture-History of the Inca Civilisation.* London: George Allen and Unwin, 1978.

[66] León-Portilla, Miguel, ed. *The Broken Spears: The Aztec Account of the Conquest of Mexico.* Boston: Beacon Press, 1990.

León-Portilla, Miguel, ed. *Fifteen Poets of the Aztec World.* Norman: University of Oklahoma Press, 1992.

[66] *Popol Vuh: The Definitive Edition of the Mayan Book of the Dawn of Life and the Glories of Gods and Kings,* with commentary based on the ancient knowledge of the Modern Quiché Maya. Trans. Dennis Tedlock. New York: Simon and Schuster, 1996.

COLONIAL CHRONICLES

[66] Betanzos, Juan de. *Narrative of the Incas.* Ed. and trans. Roland Hamilton and Dana Buchanan. Austin: University of Texas Press, 1996.

[66] Castillo, Bernal Díaz del. *The True History of the Conquest of New Spain* (1584). Trans. J. M. Cohen, in *The Conquest of New Spain.* London: Penguin Books, 1963.

[66] Cieza de León, Pedro de. *The Discovery and Conquest of Peru: Chronicles of the New World Encounter.* Ed. and trans. Alexandra Parma Cook and Noble David Cook. Durham, N.C.: Duke University Press, 1998.

[66] Cieza de León, Pedro de. *The Incas* (1547). Trans. Harriet de Onis; ed. Victor Wolfgang von Hagen. Norman: University of Oklahoma Press, 1959.

Cobo, Bernabé. *History of the Inca Empire: An Account of the Indians' Customs and Their Origin Together with a Treatise on Inca Legends, History, and Social Institutions.* Austin: University of Texas Press, 1979.

Cobo, Bernabé. *Inca Religion and Customs.* Trans. and ed. Roland Hamilton. Austin: University of Texas Press, 1989.

[66] Columbus, Ferdinand. *The Life of the Admiral Christopher Columbus by His Son Ferdinand.* Trans. Benjamin Keen. New Brunswick, N.J.: Rutgers University Press, 1992.

[66] Durán, Fray Diego. *The History of the Indies of New Spain* (1581). Trans. Doris Heyden. Norman: University of Oklahoma Press, 1994.

[66] Landa, Bishop Diego de. *Relación de las Cosas de Yucatán* (The Account of the Things of Yucatan). Ed. Alfred M. Tozzer. Papers of the Peabody Museum of Archaeology and Ethnology, Harvard University, 1941.

[66] Sahagún, Fray Bernardino de. *General History of the Things of New Spain: The Florentine Codex.* Trans. Charles E. Dibble and Arthur J. O. Anderson. Salt Lake City: University of Utah Press, 1982.

ARCHAEOLOGY

Alva, Walter, and Christopher B. Donnan. *Royal Tombs of Sipán.* Los Angeles: Fowler Museum of Cultural History, University of California, 1993.

Fash, William L. *Scribes, Warriors, and Kings: The City of Copán and the Ancient Maya.* Rev. ed. New York: Thames and Hudson, 2001.

Lourie, Peter. *The Mystery of the Maya: Uncovering the Lost City of Palenque.* Honesdale, Pa.: Boyds Mills Press, 2001.

MacDonald, Fiona. *Inca Town*. New York: Franklin Watts, 1999.

DAILY LIFE

Carrasco, David, with Scott Sessions. *Daily Life of the Aztecs: People of the Sun and Earth*. Westport, Conn.: Greenwood Press, 1998.

Calvert, Patricia. *The Ancient Inca*. New York: Franklin Watts, 2004.

Sharer, Robert J. *Daily Life in Maya Civilization*. Westport, Conn.: Greenwood Press, 1996.

RELIGION

Fisher, Leonard Everett. *Gods and Goddesses of the Ancient Maya*. New York: Holiday House, 1999.

Miller, Mary E., and Karl Taube. *An Illustrated Dictionary of the Gods and Symbols of Ancient Mexico*. New York: Thames and Hudson, 1997.

Read, Kay Almere. *A Guide to the Gods, Heroes, Rituals and Beliefs of Mexico and Central America*. New York: Oxford University Press, 2002.

SCIENCE AND TECHNOLOGY

Pringle, Heather. *The Mummy Congress: Science, Obsession, and the Everlasting Dead*. New York: Hyperion, 2002.

Reinhard, Johan. *Discovering the Inca Ice Maiden*. Washington, D.C.: National Geographic, 1998.

WRITING AND HIEROGLYPHS

Boone, Elizabeth H. *Stories in Red and Black: Pictorial Histories of the Aztecs and Mixtecs*. Austin: University of Texas Press, 2000.

Coe, Michael D. *Breaking the Maya Code*. Rev. ed. New York: Thames and Hudson, 1999.

Coulter, Laurie. *Secrets in Stone: All About Maya Hieroglyphics*. New York: Little, Brown, 2001.

Miller, Mary Ellen, and Simon Martin. *Courtly Art of the Ancient Maya*. San Francisco: Fine Arts Museums of San Francisco; New York: Thames and Hudson, 2004

Pohl, John M. D. *The Legend of Lord Eight Deer*. New York: Oxford University Press, 2002.

Quilter, Jeffrey, and Gary Urton, eds. *Narrative Threads: Accounting and Recounting in Andean Khipu*. Austin: University of Texas Press, 2002.

Solis, Felipe. *The Aztec Empire*. New York: Solomon R. Guggenheim Foundation, 2004.

WEBSITES

Archaeolink, South America
www.archaeolink.com/south_american_archaeology.htm
A comprehensive listing of links to South American cultures.

The Archaeology of the Ancient Inca Civilization
http://archaeology.about.com/od/incaarchaeology
A guide to articles and resources on the Inca.

Aztlan E-Journal
www.cc.ukans.edu/~hoopes/aztlan
An award-winning website containing full-text articles about Mesoamerica.

Exploring the Inca Heartland, Archaeological Institute of America
www.archaeology.org/online/features/peru
Map, photos, descriptions of the Inca world, and a chronology of the Spanish conquest.

The Maya Calendar, Maya World Studies Center
http://mayacalendar.com
A description of the Maya calendar and mathematical system.

Maya Ruins.com: A Photographic Tour of Sites in Mexico, Belize, Guatemala, and Honduras
http://mayaruins.com
Includes a map and information about various archaeological sites.

Maya Vase Database and Precolumbian Portfolio
www.mayavase.com
Regular and rollout photographs of artifacts and archaeological sites from various Mesoamerican cultures.

A Mesoamerican Archaeology Website
www.angelfire.com/zine/meso
A comprehensive listing of Mesoamerican archaeology links; the Precolumbian Link Page is especially good.

Mesoweb: An Exploration of Mesoamerican Cultures
www.mesoweb.com
Ask the Archaeologists (Additional Features section) for help with assignments. You can also try your luck with *The Crystal Skull* adventure game (Edutainments section).

Mundo Maya (Maya World) Online
www.mayadiscovery.com/ing/default.htm
Interesting facts about the Maya world. Find out who bought the site of Copán, in Honduras, for 50 U.S. dollars, and why a ballgame ended when one team scored just once.

Peabody Museum, Harvard University
www.peabody.harvard.edu
One of the oldest museums in the world devoted to anthropology, or the study of human culture and behavior. The Peabody Museum website has photographs of thousands of its marvelous collections of Mesoamerican and Andean textiles, pottery, shell, and metal artifacts. You can search for the artifacts from the culture of your choice.

South American Sites, Minnesota State University
www.mnsu.edu/emuseum/archaeology/sites/south.html
Photos, maps, and descriptions of important sites.

INDEX

TEXT CREDITS

MAIN TEXT

p. 17: Fray Bernardino de Sahagún, *General History of the Things of New Spain: The Florentine Codex*, Book 10, trans. Charles E. Dibble and Arthur J. O. Anderson. Salt Lake City: University of Utah Press, 1982, 51–52.

p. 17: Sahagún, *General History of the Things of New Spain*, Book 10: "The People," 41–42.

p. 19: *Popol Vuh: The Sacred Book of the Ancient Quiché Maya*. English version by Delia Goetz and Sylvanus G. Morley from Spanish translation by Adrián Recinos. Norman: University of Oklahoma Press, 1950, 167.

p. 52: *Popol Vuh*, 215–16.

p. 54: Bishop Diego de Landa, *Relación de las Cosas de Yucatán* (The Account of the Things of Yucatan), ed. Alfred M. Tozzer. Papers of the Peabody Museum of Archaeology and Ethnology, Harvard University, Vol. XVIII, 1941, 27.

p. 54: Sahagún, *General History of the Things of New Spain*, Book 8, 71.

p. 64: Ferdinand Columbus, *The Life of the Admiral Christopher Columbus by His Son Ferdinand*, trans. Benjamin Keen. New Brunswick, N. J.: Rutgers University Press, 1992, 231–32.

p. 75: Michael D. Coe, *Mexico: From the Olmecs to the Aztecs*. London: Thames and Hudson, 1994, 133.

p. 78: Fray Diego Durán, *The History of the Indies of New Spain* (1581), trans. Doris Heyden. Norman: University of Oklahoma Press, 1994.

p. 81: Durán, *The History of the Indies of New Spain*.

p. 85: Sahagún, *General History of the Things of New Spain*, Book 6.

p. 90: Bernal Díaz del Castillo, *The True History of the Conquest of New Spain* (1584), trans. J. M. Cohen, in *The Conquest of New Spain*. London: Penguin Books, 1963.

p. 94: Castillo, *The True History of the Conquest of New Spain*.

p. 95: Miguel León-Portilla, ed., *The Broken Spears: The Aztec Account of the Conquest of Mexico*. Boston: Beacon Press, 1990, 90.

p. 96: Portilla, *The Broken Spears*, 90.

p. 96: Portilla, *The Broken Spears*, 137.

p. 99: Guamán Poma, *Letters to a King*, 1567.

p. 99: Guamán Poma, *Letters to a King*, 1567, 104.

p. 100: Castillo, *The True History of the Conquest of New Spain*, 67.

p. 100: Guamán Poma, *Letters to a King*, 108.

p. 102: Guamán Poma, *Letters to a King*, 108.

p. 104: Juan de Betanzos, *Narrative of the Incas*, ed. and trans. Roland Hamilton and Dana Buchanan. Austin: University of Texas Press, 1996, 274–5.

p. 105: Pedro de Cieza de León, *The Discovery and Conquest of Peru: Chronicles of the New World Encounter*, ed. and trans. Alexandra Parma Cook and Noble David Cook. Durham, N.C.: Duke University Press, 1998, 256–57.

p. 107: Pedro de Cieza de León, *The Incas* (1547), trans. Harriet de Onis, ed. Victor Wolfgang von Hagen. Norman: University of Oklahoma Press, 1959, xli.

p. 108: Pedro de Cieza de León, *The Incas*, 20.

p. 108: Pedro de Cieza de León, *The Incas*, 44.

p. 109: Pedro de Cieza de León, *The Incas*, 303–4.

p. 127: Pedro de Cieza de León, *The Incas*, 283.

p. 130: Pedro de Cieza de León, *The Incas*, 123.

p. 140: The myth was first written down in *An Anonymous History of Trujillo*, 1604, trans. John Howland Rowe, *Acta Americana* 6, no. 1–2 (Jan.–June 1948), 26–59.

p. 149: Bernabé Cobo, *History of the Inca Empire* (1653), trans. and ed. Roland Hamilton. Austin: University of Texas Press, 1979, 134.

p. 156: Guamán Poma, *Letters to a King*, 283.

p. 156: Bernabé Cobo, *Inca Religion and Customs* (1653), trans. and ed. Roland Hamilton. Austin: University of Texas Press, 1979, 206.

SIDEBARS

p. 75: Sahagún, *General History of the Things of New Spain*, introductory vol., 38.

p. 89: Sahagún, *General History of the Things of New Spain*, Book 2.

p. 94: Castillo, *The True History of the Conquest of New Spain*.

PICTURE CREDITS

ACKNOWLEDGMENTS

I would like to thank my colleague David Carrasco for recommending me to Oxford University Press; Gary Urton, Joyce Marcus, Jeffrey Quilter, Barbara Fash, David Carrasco, and Tom Cummins for scholarly input; and my teachers over the years who instilled in me a deep appreciation of the creative genius at work in all the civilizations of the Ancient Americas. Leah Kaplan was instrumental in selecting and preparing the illustrations. Linda Ordogh deserves special recognition for all her research, compilation of sources and quotations, trips to libraries, endless photocopying and printing of documents, and a cheerful positive attitude throughout the process. Finally, I gratefully acknowledge the creativity, curiosity, and perseverance of my co-author, Mary Lyons.

—W.F.

I thank William Fash for his steady patience and sense of humor—it has been an honor to work with such a distinguished scholar. Art Collier offered his usual expert literary insights. As always, my husband, Paul Collinge, read, listened, and shared his wonderful wit.

—M.E.L.

WILLIAM FASH is Charles P. Bowditch Professor of Central American and Mexican Archaeology and Ethnology at Harvard University and director of the university's Peabody Museum. He worked on digs in Arizona and in Mexico before going to Harvard and joining Professor Gordon Willey's project in Copán, Honduras, in 1977. He and his wife, Barbara, have been working at Copán ever since, in a series of research efforts devoted to illuminating ancient Maya lifeways and cultural history. Since 1985, Professor Fash has directed the Copán Mosaics Project (succeeded in 1988 by the Copán Acropolis Archaeological Project) and most recently the Copán Sculpture Museum Project. For his efforts he was awarded Honduras's Order of José Cecilio del Valle in 1994 and was selected as Bowditch Professor at Harvard. He is the author of *Scribes, Warriors, and Kings*; *History Carved in Stone* (with Ricardo Agurcia); *Visions of the Maya Past* (with Ricardo Agurcia); and *Copán: History of an Ancient Maya City* (with E. Wyllys Andrews V).

MARY E. LYONS is a former reading specialist and school librarian. She began sharing the lost stories of southerners, women, and African Americans with her students in 1980. Now a full-time writer, she has published 17 books that include *Letters from a Slave Girl: The Story of Harriet Jacobs*; *Dear Ellen Bee: The Civil War Scrapbook of Two Union Spies*; *Knockabeg: A Famine Tale*; and *Roy Makes a Car*. Her current writing interests are Irish-American and ancient history. Lyons won the National Endowment for the Humanities Teacher-Scholar Award in 1991. In January 1998 she was writer-in-residence at Sweet Briar College, Sweet Briar, Virginia, and was a fellow-in-residence at the Virginia Center for the Humanities and Public Policy in 1991, 1993, and 1999. Lyons lives with her husband in Charlottesville, Virginia. When she is not researching or writing books, she plays banjo and penny whistle with the Chicken Heads, a traditional music group. Their motto is "We Play for Chicken Feed." For more information, visit *www.lyonsdenbooks.com*.

RONALD MELLOR, who is professor of history at UCLA, first became enthralled with ancient history as a student at Regis High School in New York City. He is the statewide faculty advisor of the California History–Social Science Project (CHSSP), which brings university faculty together with K-12 teachers at sites throughout California. In 2000, the American Historical Association awarded the CHSSP the Albert J. Beveridge Award for K-12 teaching. Professor Mellor has held fellowships from the National Endowment for the Humanities and the American Council of Learned Societies. His research has centered on ancient religion and Roman historiography. His books include *Theia Rhome: The Goddess Roma in the Greek World* (1975); *From Augustus to Nero: The First Dynasty of Imperial Rome* (1990); *Tacitus* (1993); *Tacitus: The Classical Heritage* (1995); *The Historians of Ancient Rome* (1997); and *The Roman Historians* (2nd edition, 2004).

AMANDA PODANY is a specialist in the history of the ancient Near East and a professor of history at California State Polytechnic University, Pomona. She has taught there since 1990 and is currently serving as the director of the university's honors program. From 1993 to 1997 she was executive director of the California History–Social Science Project, a professional development program for history–social science teachers at all grade levels. Her work in professional development for teachers has received major grants from the California Postsecondary Education Commission and the United States Department of Education. Her publications include *The Land of Hana: Kings, Chronology, and Scribal Tradition*. Professor Podany has also published numerous journal articles on ancient Near Eastern history and on approaches to teaching. She lives in Los Angeles with her husband and two children.